Army Fundamentals

Army Fundamentals

From Making Soldiers to the Limits of the Military Instrument

Edited by B. K. Greener

MASSEY UNIVERSITY PRESS

MASSEY
UNIVERSITY
PRESS

First published in 2017 by Massey University Press
Private Bag 102904, North Shore Mail Centre
Auckland 0745, New Zealand
www.masseypress.ac.nz

Design by Kate Barraclough

A catalogue record for this book is available from the National Library of New Zealand

Printed and bound in China by Everbest

ISBN: 978-0-9941407-3-9
eISBN: 978-0-9941407-4-6

Contents

Foreword

NEW ZEALAND IS CURRENTLY RANKED the fourth most peaceful country in a most truculent, threatening and testing world. As I have often remarked, New Zealand's location is best described as a geostrategic punctuation mark on Antarctica. We have the great fortune of being a strategic irrelevance to most of the tectonic clashes of our age or any other. Looking out at this brutish world, most New Zealanders are often conflicted. On the one hand, colonial and Pacific immigrant roots underpin a culture that sees itself as inevitably and rightly part of the world, reflecting the history of how New Zealanders came to be on these islands. We are a nation that is internationally oriented, with the non-threatening attractiveness of a 'small but useful' power status. But our internationalism also reflects a strongly held sense so well expressed in John Donne's 'Meditation 17':

> No man is an island entire of itself; every man is a piece of the continent, a part of the main; if a clod be washed away by the sea, Europe is the less, as well as if a promontory were, as well as any manner of thy friends or of thine own were; any man's death diminishes me, because I am involved in mankind. And therefore never send to know for whom the bell tolls; it tolls for thee.

On the other hand, the very same smallness of New Zealand's national power; the domestic demands upon a narrow and fragile national economy; our geostrategic isolation; and a disgust and frustration with the inhumanity, political failures and dismal human and material costs of war have all contributed to a New Zealand that often wants to leave the rest of the world to its own devices, and feels it can.

Military forces (army, navy and air force), as a national instrument of power in New Zealand's relations with the rest of the world, reflect this vacillation: surviving through times of indifference to downright culpable neglect alternates with times of eager and overly generous commitment to the resolution of regional and even global conflicts. National decisions to divert treasure and talent to constructing and maintaining competent, professional and capable military forces reflect a minimalist realism: 'we would rather not, but if and when we have to, we will'.

This on-again, off-again approach to diverting national resources for defence forces only in times when extreme and urgent need is undeniable has never really worked. During the more clearly distinguishable periods of peace and war it stumbled along, justifying extremely small professional forces, almost as a yeast 'starter culture' from which to dramatically expand in the event of an outbreak of war. Since New Zealand's contribution, in and of itself, could never be of a size to make a material difference to the outcome, there would always be time to mobilise and train up citizen armies and, after the event, to demob and return soldiers to their civilian status once more.

However, the contemporary state of international relations, characterised by the persistent violent conflict and continuing instability that characterise this re-emergent era of aspirant great powers, stands quite at odds with outdated mobilisation strategies. The complexities, risks and challenges of today's conflicts, and the sophisticated leader and soldier skill sets demanded by them, make quickly mobilising civilian armies impractical and imprudent. As US Secretary of Defense Rumsfeld is often quoted: 'You go with the army you have — not the army you might want or wish to have at a later time.'

However outdated, mobilisation strategies have allowed New Zealand, in a comparative sense, to maintain exceedingly low levels of national expenditure on defence forces, and to maintain extremely small military forces particularly over the past half-century. For example, using 2014 International Institute for Strategic Studies data for active forces per 1000 capita, New Zealand is ranked 116th out of 170-odd countries. Interestingly, of the three countries higher on the Global Peace Index, only Iceland, a founding member of the North Atlantic Treaty Organization (NATO), has fewer forces, ranked at 168th. By comparison, Fiji is ranked 67th in the world, the United States 50th, Russia 29th, and Singapore 10th.

I use these figures not just to help out with a game of Trivial Pursuit. With only two members of the armed forces for every 1000 people, it is almost inevitable that the overwhelming bulk of New Zealanders have little to no understanding of, or interaction with, their armed forces. As the New Zealand Defence Force has contracted its basing footprint over the last decades, fewer NZDF members are located near or in major concentrations of the population. Moreover, as the Second World War and 1950s generations of veterans pass away, and given that conscripted service ended in the 1960s, there are simply (and, in a way, thankfully) fewer and fewer New Zealanders with experience of military and war service.

The consequence of these policy choices and historical circumstances, as the editor and authors of this work so well point out, is that today most New Zealanders — and that includes most national leaders — do not really know their armed forces. Fewer national and local leaders have critical knowledge of national security and military affairs sufficient to guide their interactions with professional military advisors. Despite the sound work of individuals, the country lacks a pluralism of credible, objective, balanced strategic-level national security and military policy advice options to balance those provided by military leaderships. This has led to periods of intensely dependent or alternatively suspicious and distrusting relationships between political and military leaderships, with poor outcomes for resourcing and developing military forces fitted to mission and to how missions are likely to evolve in the future.

This multi-authored work adds to our national knowledge about New Zealand's armed forces — in this case, the New Zealand Army — in a most timely way, since there is a critical need for other ways, such as this volume, to share understanding about the profession of arms and the demands and challenges of its societally unique mission. A mission that, unlike any other civic task (even those of other first responders, such as police and fire-fighters), involves the taking and sacrificing of life itself to protect and defend the security of the nation.

Greener and her team of researchers and writers delve into some of the seemingly idiosyncratic aspects of the New Zealand Army's culture, value system, enculturation practices and operational learning with vignettes, case studies and observations that help explain military purpose, action and effect. They do so in a rich, multi-perspective approach that draws on multiple social science disciplines. In this way, they help show how the New Zealand Army's traditions, practices and values seek to fit its members to cope, survive and succeed in contemporary operational settings.

They also raise a number of critical issues of military life, such as the preparation for and undertaking of military missions that have been created or exacerbated by limited knowledge and short-sighted strategic policy around our defence forces. Most particularly, for example, the 'No. 8 fencing wire' approach that has for too long relied upon gifted improvisation to compensate for short-changed resourcing. While making improvised grenades from bully-beef tins, gun cotton and nails can be looked back on with a certain measure of pride, it is no recipe for equipping and training military forces for the low-tech and high-tech, moral and legal quagmires that characterise future war.

Equally, the authors place a spotlight on the extent to which the New Zealand Army has, in common with many other Western military forces, become the convenient go-to force for myriad crises, conflicts and state collapses that run well beyond the scope of traditional war. They recognise the failure to develop national and international strategies for conflict mitigation and reconstruction that integrate, balance and properly resource diplomatic, smart-tech, economic and military governmental and non-governmental contributions. They seek to provide a warning: while New Zealand society and its governmental leaders continue to rely on the adaptability of the New Zealand Army and its sister services to cover the territory, in the absence of compensatory resourcing, this strategy stretches the elasticity of a military force to and beyond a breaking point. And there are inevitable consequences.

Army Fundamentals opens the watch-face to show us some of the internal workings of the New Zealand Army. It also offers multiple perspectives on the social, demographic, economic and national cultural factors that are shaping the army's current and future workforce. Its vignettes and case studies highlight the internal conflicts that its leaders must manage adroitly between its proven traditions and practices and the evolving social culture from which it must always draw its legitimacy. Finally, it puts the New Zealand context on the ongoing tensions faced by military leaders. These tensions involve designing and preparing military forces as uniformed, disciplined and armed 'maids of all work', while at the same time preparing for and conducting traditional tactical combat and combat support missions. In this, the authors and editors have done us a great service.

Cathy Downes PhD

Professor, US National Defense University

The views expressed are those of the author and do not reflect the official policy or position of the US National Defense University, the US Department of Defense, or the US Government.

Introducing Army Fundamentals

B. K. Greener

IN HIS DISCUSSION OF THE military, the famous Prussian strategist Carl von Clausewitz argued that government must know 'the instrument it means to use' (1976: 607). He expected that political leaders would either have direct relevant military experience themselves, or that they would have access to military advice in deciding how this military instrument could potentially be put to use in furthering the political interests of the state. This assumption that policy-makers have access to sound military advice and that, through this advice, they know something about what militaries are and what they can do may hold true. However, outside of such privileged positions, most civilians don't necessarily have a clear idea about exactly what contemporary militaries are and what they do. Nor do military personnel necessarily comprehend how they are perceived by those outside of the disciplined forces.

How, then, might those interested in national and international politics, military forces, or the use of military force more generally, better come to know this 'military instrument', especially given the purposeful separation of professional all-volunteer military forces from society in modern liberal democracies?

This book examines one such military instrument: the New Zealand Army. It aims to disseminate knowledge and ideas about military identity and military functions to help encourage informed debate about defence and security matters. It aims to help bridge the theory–practice divide in attempting to better understand, explain and critique the nature and work of militaries. This book also seeks to hold up a mirror to military personnel to help increase understanding about how the nature and work of this institution might be understood from a variety of insider and outsider perspectives. It is hoped, too, that this work might help to improve civil–military relations, to potentially boost operational effectiveness, and to increase overall political and social comprehension of such matters in the public sphere. Complementary to the call of the New Zealand Defence White Paper (NZ MoD 2016a: 65) for the New Zealand Defence Force (NZDF) to both be flexible and 'fit for purpose', this book seeks to ask just what the New Zealand Army is and what it does.

Why a book on the New Zealand Army?

THE RESEARCH PRESENTED HERE FIRST of all seeks to spur increased interest and informed discussion about defence and security matters in the New Zealand setting. Within New Zealand there have long been calls for more robust public debate about security and defence matters. However, with rather small academic, journalistic and NGO communities to call upon, this debate has been somewhat limited both in reach and in sites of participation. Importantly, the undertaking of this endeavour also broadens the national debate by moving beyond the usual suspects. This edited collection brings together work by exciting new scholars, current practitioners and established academics in examining the identity and functions of the New Zealand Army from a wider range of perspectives than has occurred in previous work. Drawing from anthropology, political studies, international relations, development studies, law, education and defence and security studies, as well as from personal anecdotes and experiences, this text provides a multi-faceted view of one military organisation in order to further our understanding about the various components of, and challenges to, the character of military personnel, institutions and ascribed activities in the twenty-first century. The focus on the army, rather than the NZDF (which also includes the air force and the navy), is predominantly due to the scale both of the institution under scrutiny (the army is the largest — almost twice as large as the air force or navy) and of this project.

For those who are not *au fait* with New Zealand as a country, it is a small island nation whose strategic culture is affected significantly by its isolated location. With no land borders, an ally (Australia) as the closest neighbour, a large maritime estate, interests in Antarctica and significant political, economic and military commitments in the South Pacific in particular, New Zealand exists in a somewhat luxurious security situation. The country is developed, relatively affluent, and export-driven, with a small population of just over four million residents. Recent years have seen a renewed political relationship with the United States through the Washington and Wellington Declarations, alongside an ever-growing trade relationship with China.

It is within this setting — one where consecutive Defence White Papers have said that there is no direct military threat to New Zealand — that the small but professional New Zealand Army originates. Nonetheless, owing in part to the isolation, the importance of export and trade, and previous colonial then US alliance-oriented ties, the New Zealand Army has also been very active in international affairs. Its structures and organisational features mimic those of other Western nations, and indeed New Zealand's defence diplomacy and other relationships with the UK, US, Canada and Australia have remained important through turbulent times.

This brings us to the potential for a broader contribution to be made by this volume. There is a need for further research to help better understand the internal nature of militaries in an era of complexity, the changing identities of soldiers, and the evolving functions of modern volunteer militaries within democratic societies. The rising importance of the issue of gender, the consequences of adopting UNSC resolutions which centre on the protection of civilians in undertaking peace and stability operations, and the increased use of militaries outside of their core functions when deployed abroad demand a closer examination of just what militaries are and what they do. Moreover, for the present time, sources on these issues are currently limited and are predominantly focused on American experiences. New Zealand therefore provides a 'similar yet different' case for consideration.

Existing work

RESEARCH ON CIVIL–MILITARY RELATIONS AND the place of military force and of military forces is typically military sociology-focused, and often considers the unique case of the US. Leaping off from seminal work by authors such as Samuel Huntington (*The Soldier and the State*), Samuel Finer (*The Man on Horseback*) and Morris Janowitz (*The Professional Soldier*), this body of literature looks at the political and strategic nature of the relationship between political masters and military leadership in liberal democratic societies (see also the more recent work of Cohen 1995 and 2002, Moskos [ed.] et al. 1999, Desch 2001, Feaver 2003, Schiff 2009, and the edited collections by Caforio 2003 and Bruneau and Matei 2013). Other research of this ilk focuses on the likelihood or consequences of military coups in developing states (see, for example, Barany 2012) or the overall militarisation of society and the consequences of militarism (see Enloe 2000; 2007 and Teaiwa 2008). The question of the potential role of military forces in political matters is thus a broad one, and a fundamentally important one too, but there is a disconnect between this macro-level view of how military institutions and personnel — those that have the capacity to use lethal force — 'fit' in liberal democratic states, and some of the more micro-level studies that have been done on the actual work that militaries do.

Another type of literature — often to be found in places such as the journal *Armed Forces and Society* — therefore focuses on specific and often more operational issues. This category of research includes work on topics such as recruitment, retention and attrition rates, addressing post-traumatic stress disorder, the role of reservists, or the consequences of gender integration. This type of literature comes from a variety of fields of study, such as anthropology, defence studies, development studies, economics, gender studies, international relations, leadership studies, management, peace studies, politics, psychology and sociology. Of greatest relevance to this text are those works that consider issues of operational matters in the light of broader strategic objectives and the difficulties in achieving political purposes via military means (see, for example, Egnell 2009 and Reveron 2010). Another particularly relevant research area is that which analyses the changing roles of militaries in providing internal security in contemporary times (see Edmund 2006, Dandeker 2010, and Schnabel and Krupanski 2012).

Caforio's (2007) edited collection *Social Sciences and the Military* comes closest to the aims of this book. It brings together culture, social history, organisational aesthetics, psychology, political science and other approaches to the field in seeking to promote what Caforio calls 'interdisciplinary and cross-national' studies of the military. He argues that such approaches are necessary due to the complexity of issues at play for contemporary military forces. However, no book has yet drawn on such different disciplinary research approaches in examining *one particular* military institution in an attempt to provide a more thorough and multi-faceted account of the nature, form and function of one of these modern military instruments at play in a liberal democracy today. Moreover, Caforio's edited collection is aimed at scholars and is therefore a little impenetrable for some readers. This text seeks a different, albeit complementary, path to that encouraged by Caforio.

In terms of existing sources on the New Zealand case, the closest pieces of research are to be found in the work of Downes (2000), on the changing roles of military forces in both New Zealand and Australia in the post-cold war era; Ayson (2004), on the potentially cosmopolitan nature of the NZDF; Rolfe (1999), who considers the profile, policy and structures of the New Zealand defence sector and who also provides an overview of the main characteristics of the army in an encyclopaedia entry (2015); [Peter] Greener (2009), on political and bureaucratic decision-making in the NZDF's defence acquisitions; [Bethan] Greener and Fish (2015), on security provision in peace and stability operations, drawing on New Zealand and Australian experiences; and Hoadley (2015), on civil–military relations in New Zealand's deployment to Afghanistan. Additional works that comment on particular operational deployments are to be found in the work of military historians such as Glyn Harper (see, for example, 2011; 2012; 2015; 2016) and John Crawford (see, for example, Crawford 1996; Crawford and Harper 2001), as well as in various defence papers and books by military personnel themselves (such as Hayward 2003; Hall 2010; Dransfield 2016). Room remains, however, for a more comprehensive consideration of this subject.

In this new text, then, it is hoped that we not only give an in-depth view of a particular case study in examining the New Zealand Army, but also that we might provide some insight into broader international issues. Moreover, in keeping with the aims of increasing participation in this discussion, the authors have attempted to minimise jargon while retaining a robust academic approach.

Structure of the book

ARMY FUNDAMENTALS **FOCUSES ON TWO** main themes: identity and function. The early chapters focus predominantly on identity, though these demonstrate that military identities are also tied up with core institutional functions.

Harding's chapter opens this volume with a discussion about how soldiers are made. Focusing on one particular incident — the 'incident with the door' — Harding demonstrates how soldiers are trained to internalise a certain set of 'dispositions' such that leaving a door unsecured would be seen to warrant — indeed demand — a form of punishment. These dispositions are taken on by recruits as they physically act out certain tasks, and, in doing so, take on guiding principles that become second nature. Having identified the army's official emphasis on the four values of Courage, Comradeship, Commitment and Integrity, Harding formulates that there are (at least) four dispositions which soldiers take on in responding to these values: *security, attention to detail, sense of urgency,* and *get over it.* She explores these dispositions, as well as the overarching emphasis on being 'switched on', in coming to the conclusion that soldiering emphasises the ability to 'do' and to be ready for action, before finally reminding us that failing to secure a door demonstrates a failure to internalise these dispositions properly.

Guesgen's chapter dovetails neatly into Harding's work and is similar in its anthropological focus which emphasises the importance of culture. Instead of considering how soldiers are made, however, Guesgen looks at the *unmaking* of officer cadets. That is, she demonstrates how a particular cohort of officer cadets — known as 'Kippenbergers', or 'Kipps' — had not undergone the same sorts of processes that soldier recruits had, such that an individual officer was outraged, rather than resigned, at being punished for leaving a door unsecured (hence 'the incident with the door'). As part of an attempt to attract a certain sort of recruit into the officer corps, the army had instituted a scheme whereby it would pay for university fees and in return (or so went the thinking) receive educated and committed officers. Guesgen's chapter suggests, however, that this was always going to be difficult. The social setting for these cadets was a neoliberal environment that emphasised 'user pays', the rolling back of the state, and the primacy of the marketplace. It was also an environment in which a new generation was experiencing high levels of individual autonomy, high rates of individual responsibility and a strong economy, which meant that the army had to compete with a range of employers who often offered experiences more in keeping with generational expectations. Given these contextual influences, and the confusion created by exposure to both university culture and military culture at the same time, some Kipps struggled to adapt when castigated for leaving a door unsecured.

A strong capacity for adaptation is, however, a vital part of modern military forces. Morris's chapter brings together these key themes of identity and function in discussing how military personnel deployed to the Provincial Reconstruction Team (PRT) in Bamiyan province, Afghanistan, coped with undertaking non-core tasks. Adding to the literature on the military's role in development, Morris asks how personnel coped with being tasked with performing developmental rather than security roles. She suggests that, being less able to adopt a more traditional form of 'Anzac' identity, these personnel instead drew on a military identity with the more recent emphasis on 'professionalism'. As professionals, these personnel were aware of the need to know more about the development field in which they found themselves working. This augurs well in signalling a willingness to adapt and improve, but also signals caution in that — as later chapters show — moving away from 'core business' is a complicated matter.

Developing her theme of identity, Morris emphasises that the professed professionalism of the New Zealand Army is something in which its personnel take pride. Peter Greener's chapter evaluates this further, suggesting that the view may have some merit outside of popular opinion. Drawing on interviews with other military and civilian personnel who have served alongside New Zealand troops, Greener demonstrates that, overall, Kiwi peacekeepers may deserve at least some of the laurels thrown their way. Personnel from other countries confirm the professionalism, humility and general attitude of New Zealand personnel. However, certain areas for improvement are highlighted — there is, after all, a difference between cultural appreciation (which most Kiwis seem to have) and cultural competence (which is a learned skill that requires additional input). One way of fostering cultural competence might be to ensure that military personnel do not have to add *other* tasks to their training manuals and 'to do' lists.

This brings us back to the case of Afghanistan. Lauren's chapter draws on observations and interviews conducted during a visit to the Kiwi PRT. It brings together some of the themes raised by Morris and Greener in a more conversational piece that considers some of the operating environments, tasks and ways in which personnel were viewed by others. Lauren voices concerns about requiring personnel to undertake a range of tasks that they do not feel fully equipped to do, as well as confirming the notion that — on the whole — NZDF personnel are viewed positively. However, he also asks how such commitments can be successfully concluded, and highlights some of the consequences of deploying armed military personnel.

The impact of using armed personnel is a theme that resurfaces in the following chapter, by Stevens and Beth Greener, which explores how military personnel themselves, as well as those they interact with in operational settings, understand their work, its impacts, and their identity and motivating values. Focusing on the deployment to the Solomon Islands, the authors draw on another aspect that contributes to military identity: gender. As noted above, some of the existing literature on military forces emphasises militarisation — particularly with respect to a perceived 'hyper-masculinity' of military forces (see Whitworth 2004; 2005; and Sjoberg 2013). This body of work helps us to begin to understand what is valued by personnel and how some of those more militarised values may be unhelpful in attempts to undertake conflict resolution. Stevens and Greener also raise the broader question of how militaries and masculinity intersect to place value on armed responses to security situations.

Derbyshire's chapter also discusses gender, albeit in a different way. It begins with a personal reflection demonstrating the more nuanced form of gender discrimination that occurs within military settings — discrimination stemming from the society that houses the military institution in question. Noting that New Zealand has a relatively strong track record in terms of gender equality and equity, Derbyshire outlines additional moves undertaken in response to external initiatives (such as UNSC Resolution 1325), to increasing recognition of the importance of female personnel, and to rising retention problems within the army itself. Derbyshire suggests areas for improvement, beginning with the notion of rethinking and reconstituting what we understand to be the epitome of a 'modern warrior'.

The chapter by Wineera continues this theme of improvement. That is, he considers both how and why New Zealand has sought to engage in Building Partner Capacity programmes to help improve others' military capabilities (such as in the current BPC programme under way in Iraq), as well as considering how the army has sought to improve its own delivery of such training and mentoring programmes. Drawing on literature on security sector reform (SSR) as well as that from adult education, Wineera outlines how New Zealand personnel have recently sought to adapt their own learning and teaching practices. Speaking again to the themes of adaptability and professionalism, he notes some interesting recent developments regarding the uptake of new approaches to understanding the work of the army when engaged in capacity building.

The final chapter is a collaborative effort in which Fish, Beth Greener, Harding and Sigley conclude some of the themes raised earlier by considering the limits of military action. Leaping off from a philosophical approach, they address some commonly expressed assumptions about military personnel. Certain sacred cows such as 'the best warfighters make the best peacekeepers' and 'you can always ramp down but you can't always ramp up' contribute to the notion that military personnel 'can' undertake a wide range of tasks, from combat all the way down the spectrum of operations. But can they?

Having opened with von Clausewitz, the book returns in this final chapter to that demi-god of strategic thought in noting that one of the important roles of senior military personnel is to provide advice to political masters. In particular, the authors assert that such advice must increasingly emphasise when the capacity and reach of the military instrument has been exhausted, or will be exhausted should a suggested act be undertaken. Yet, to do this, senior military personnel must follow the injunction to 'know thyself', understand the nature of their own institution, and be able to communicate the limits of this 'military instrument' to those who make policy in order to mitigate risk and to increase chances of military and political success.

This book sets out to engage and inform insiders and outsiders on military personnel, culture, institutions and the use of military force in general. It aims to introduce the reader to a variety of views about what the New Zealand Army is and does. Readers may or may not agree with its conclusions; but if it helps to increase levels of understanding, interest and information about the topic across a range of individuals and institutions, then, we believe, this book has achieved its primary goal.

01

Locking in a Military Identity: Making soldiers

N. Harding

AT THE SAME TIME THAT I was writing my PhD at Massey University on the process of becoming a soldier in the New Zealand Army, another postgraduate student in my department (Guesgen, this volume) was doing a similar project on the process of becoming an officer in the same army. We had the same supervisor, who one day mentioned that the trainee soldiers ('recruits') with whom I was working seemed to act quite differently from the trainee officers ('cadets') with whom my colleague was working. In particular, one of Guesgen's informants told her that the third year of his cadet training had been 'crap' because 'I kept getting charged for stupid things like leaving my door unlocked'.

A charge is a kind of military punishment; not one of first resort, but rather a serious and formal reprimand. In this case such charges meant that the cadet was repeatedly confined to barracks for periods of three weeks. 'Leaving my door unlocked' refers to forgetting to lock his bedroom door when he left barracks, something required by a formal written order. The story itself, from the perspective of the cadet, will be told in the next chapter. What I want to build on in this chapter is my reaction to this story: I was shocked.

My informants would never have told a researcher that their training was 'crap' because of such a punishment. This is because 1) they would not conceptualise accidentally leaving their bedroom door unlocked as a 'stupid thing' to be punished for, and 2) even if they had, they wouldn't have said so out loud to a civilian. I think most civilians, like the cadet in question, would consider a charge to be a harsh consequence for a minor mistake, and, before I was embedded with a group of new recruits for my PhD research, I probably would have too. But I myself, along with one of my informants, was once punished for not locking a bedroom door, and we did then — as I do now — believe that we deserved it. Leaving a door unlocked seems like a trivial incident, and yet it takes on great significance during the process of becoming a soldier. Recruits who made this mistake would interpret it as a sign that they had not yet managed to fully internalise the soldier identity, something in which they are highly invested.

Drawing on theorist Pierre Bourdieu's (1977; 1990) theory of practice, in which identity is seen to be shaped by a set of habitual inclinations and transposable tendencies ('habitus'), I will explain both why my informants accepted that they deserved punishment for such infractions and why they would never publicly complain in any case. The inculcation of both of these responses in recruits further socialised them in practices that are effective in the field and on deployment. In this way I will explore how not only this particular small aspect of everyday life but *every* small aspect of everyday life was enrolled in the project of turning civilians into soldiers.

My direct experience of the significance of leaving a door unlocked during military training is a result of the anthropological method of participant observation. Participant observation involves living amongst the community of interest and, as far as possible, experiencing life in the way that they experience it, and this is the method by which I collected the data on which this chapter is based. The primary aim of this approach is to attempt to more fully grasp the informants' own understanding of the topic in question: through experiencing what they experience, 'we can come to interpret the world more or less in the same way that they do' (Hammersley and Atkinson 2007: 8).

Thus in my case I wanted to understand the identity transition from civilian to soldier from the recruits' own point of view, and to do this I was embedded with a cohort of new soldiers for the first year and a half of their career in the New Zealand Army. This involved following them through four different stages of their training and career, but as this chapter is about *making* soldiers, it focuses solely on the first of these stages, Basic Training. Basic (pronounced 'BASSick' not 'BAYsick') is the first stage of training for all soldiers regardless of occupational speciality, and it teaches core soldier competencies such as weapons handling, communications, navigation, first aid, field-craft and drill. It is here that recruits take on a military identity and become soldiers.

I was embedded with one platoon for the duration of Basic Training, and initially intended to train with the recruits as much as possible. However, I very quickly partially paralysed my left arm and was relegated to the 'observation' side of participant observation for physical training. But I could still participate in what is referred to as 'barracks routine', which is, basically, everyday living. The platoon was often told, 'You're at Basic to learn the basics,' and when the army says the basics, it really means the basics. The first few weeks of Basic consisted of learning how to dress ourselves, get ourselves to places on time, keep military kit in order, and achieve all of this without leaving the barracks in a mess. In order to attempt to understand the recruits' experience, I had to follow all orders, move within barracks and other spaces as the recruits did ('doubling' — running, rather than walking) and, in front of recruits, interact with the NCOs (non-commissioned officers) and platoon commander in the same way that they did (using rank, coming to attention). I shared responsibility for fatigues (cleaning) within barracks, and I wore a uniform, although it was a different cut and camouflage to the ones the recruits wore, so people could tell me apart. Thus during barracks and uniform inspections I was inspected with everyone else.

Platoons are made up of three sections of 10 to 12 soldiers each, and bedrooms in barracks are assigned by section. This meant there was one male bedroom per section, and then one bedroom for the females of all sections. At this time there were four female recruits in our platoon. I did not sleep in the platoon's barracks with them, but rather in the officers' mess, for ethical reasons: essentially, living somewhere else meant that the female soldiers didn't have to be around a researcher 24/7. However, I also had a 'bedspace' in the female bedroom to use and be inspected on during the day. The bedrooms consisted of rows of such bedspaces, each consisting of a single bed and a tallboy, in which each recruit lived, stored all of their kit and demonstrated their ability to follow army regulations.

Leaving the door unlocked at Basic Training

THE INCIDENT WITH THE DOOR occurred in the early evening, before dinner. The platoon had just returned to barracks from the rifle range, where the recruits had spent a long day participating in weapons qualifications. Most of the platoon were cleaning their rifles but 'Miller' (a female recruit) and I, who were both injured, had not fired any weapons that day. Instead we were doing laundry for the other female recruits. We fetched their washing from the bedroom and ran down to the laundry room, unthinkingly leaving the bedroom door open behind us. The rest of the platoon, 30-odd people, were sitting lined up along both sides of the corridor, not three metres away from the open bedroom door, so it was not as if anybody could have wandered in to steal anything without being seen. However, we should have known better than to leave the room 'insecure'.

Right from the start we had been taught to always close and lock the door behind us whenever we left the room empty. At one point very early in Basic Training, when everything was new and overwhelming and it still felt as if we couldn't do anything right, I recorded in my field notes that the platoon had 'gone really hard' at fatigues that day, and thought we had 'done awesome', but found that this effort had been completely undermined by two of the rooms having been left with their doors insecure. Because the mistake of any member of a training platoon is considered the mistake of everybody (in order to encourage recruits to help bring one another up to standard), we were not told which rooms had been left insecure. 'We think one was us,' my field notes say. The fact that we couldn't recall if we had shut our door in the frantic rush to be on the parade ground ready for dinner in immaculate uniform, having left immaculate barracks behind us, showed that we were still acting like civilians rather than attentive soldiers. In the same month, other recruits who had left rooms and/or wardrobes insecure had at various times returned to barracks to discover their clothing decorating trees. A few days later, I recorded that we had lately had a much better knowledge of 'the state of our door'.

This was, however, apparently wishful thinking on my and Miller's behalf. By the time we had once again left the door open a few weeks later, we shouldn't have still been having issues with 'the basics'. Blissfully ignorant, we set the washing machines going and came back into the corridor, where the whole platoon had fallen into a palpable silence. Each recruit was warily concentrating on the weapons part they were cleaning and carefully listening to some obvious *thumps*. The other girls whispered to us: 'He's hurricaning the room.'

'He' was 'Sir', the platoon commander, and to 'hurricane' the room is to put it into a state that would make you think a hurricane had hit it. He was tossing the bedroom, throwing the mattresses and their bedding off the bed bases, and so forth — a fairly basic hurricaning to reflect the junior status of the recruits. Eventually Sir came out, looked at me and Miller, standing ineffectually in the corridor with our laundry bags, and asked, 'What's the implied task if your room is left insecure?' Not met with any acceptable answer, he roared, 'Secure it!' We sprinted into the room and locked the door behind us, our one goal to restore the room to order before the other girls were released from weapons cleaning.

Why should I tell this potentially boring story about a door? Why did no one blink an eye at a punishment for something that may seem trivial or, in the words of the cadet above, 'stupid'? And why do movies and other popular culture representations of recruit training often focus on such small, everyday aspects of barracks life, when there are so many more exciting aspects to becoming a soldier? The answer to all of the above is that, in the context of Basic Training, small things such as leaving a door unlocked, far from being inconsequential, are in fact imbued with great significance.

A transposable soldier habitus

COMMON DISCOURSE AMONGST ACADEMICS AND civilians seems to be that the military's control over the basic aspects of everyday life is debasing to those who submit to it (Burke 2004: xiv). This goes along with a common adage in which it is assumed that military training 'systematically breaks down recruits and rebuilds them into soldiers' (Gill 2009: 144).

For example, although Burke, like me, sees the basic tasks of everyday living as highly significant, she argues that the fact that the military 'control[s] every minute of the recruits' days' is 'infantiliz[ing]' (13). She writes that militaries

> deliberately treat the recruits as children, scolding these babes in arms because in the eyes of the institution they do not speak properly, walk properly, or even eat properly. They cannot accomplish even the simplest of tasks — making the bed or cleaning the floor — to the satisfaction of their overseers (25–6).

The recruits with whom I was embedded in the New Zealand Army, however, did not see it this way.

From the recruits' point of view, the army wasn't breaking them down to build them back up, but rather was just building them up. They had joined the army for the very purpose of changing their identity, and they wanted it to be a real challenge in which they could improve their capabilities, and hence selves, through facing and conquering hardship. They didn't view being punished for the state of their bedroom as akin to being chastised like naughty or incompetent children, but rather as providing them with part of this desired challenge. Making a bed and cleaning the floor to army standards is not 'simple'. The recruits saw these as skills they did not yet have but which they would acquire in order to prove themselves. It was not when staff yelled at them and tossed their rooms that they complained, but rather when they *didn't*: 'Sergeant seems too soft'; 'Sarge is a bit too relaxed'. About the platoon commander who did toss rooms they said: 'Sir is awesome', 'Sir's cool, eh'.

Small everyday tasks were significant in the context of Basic Training not only because failure to complete them earned punishment, or because this meant that you had let others down (as was the case with the other girls, who had their room trashed through no fault of their own). It was also because failure to properly execute everyday tasks was explicitly conflated with *failure to act as a soldier would*, and hence a failure to fully internalise the soldier identity.

The New Zealand Army sees the process of becoming a soldier as the internalisation of army values by each individual recruit. The recruits are then to 'self-lead' in line with these values in all areas of their lives:

> The ethos and values of the NZ Army become an integral part of a soldier's own value system and sense of who they are. Thus they act in accordance with these even when under significant duress or in an environment inconsistent with them (Horn et al. 2008: 29).

Army values internalised during Basic Training are to be 'the basis for your decision-making in the absence of external direction' (New Zealand

Defence Force 2009b: 20) and 'must now serve as your guides when considering what is appropriate in any situation — whether you are in uniform or not' (ibid. 2009c: 2). Thus what the army is trying to achieve is the socialisation of soldiers who will of their own volition act in ways that are deemed most effective for soldiers without needing to be ordered to do so. These ways of acting are fundamentally important to the role of soldiering. They are to become second nature so that they are not forgotten in the stress and chaos of battle, and so that soldiers will act in these ways everywhere they find themselves, even in situations that might encourage other sorts of behaviour.

The army uses the word 'values' for the ways in which it wants its soldiers to act, and specifically identifies these values as Courage, Comradeship, Commitment and Integrity (3CI). Although 'values' is a noun that connotes what people think and believe rather than how they act, the army sees values as primarily guides to *action*: they 'are only useful if the behaviours which make up the values are acted on by all members of the Army on a day to day basis' (NZ Army 2013: 32). In recognising the importance of values as actions, Bourdieu's concepts of 'habitus' and 'dispositions' can help me to make further sense of what is really going on here.

Understanding how soldiers are made

AS SEEN ABOVE, THE ARMY conceptualises soldier identity ('a soldier's [. . .] sense of who they are') primarily through actions, ways of behaving that Bourdieu (1977) would call 'durable' (long-lasting) and 'transposable' (enacted in all spheres rather than being context specific) (72). Bourdieu's concept of habitus and its role in identity formation focuses on how we act. This therefore is a suitable theory not only in terms of attempting to understand the army as an institution but also in terms of attempting to better understand the soldiers themselves, who see their identity in terms of how many push-ups they can do and what new challenges they can conquer.

Habitus is a concept that argues that 'the most fundamental structures of the group' are 'root[ed]' in 'the primary experiences of the body' (Bourdieu 1990: 71). That is, soldier habitus physically grounds army requirements in each individual soldier as muscle memory.

An individual's habitus provides 'procedures to follow, paths to take' (53) and produces 'a durable way of standing, speaking, walking, and thereby of feeling and thinking' (70). A habitus is made up of dispositions, 'inclination[s]' and 'tendenc[ies]' (Bourdieu cited in Bourdieu and Passeron 1990: 68, fn1).

Our dispositions are the ways in which we are predisposed to act and react to events around us. We don't have to think about our dispositions consciously; because they are rooted in the body we just act on them. Although socialised rather than innate, they work similarly to instincts. At some point we learned them, but they have become 'second nature' (Bourdieu 1990: 56) to us. This explains how it is that they are transposable: we carry them with us wherever we go and hence are predisposed to act in the same ways in whatever diverse contexts we find ourselves in. It is these habitual unconscious behaviour patterns that are seen to shape our identities.

In explaining this further, it is helpful to be clear on the exact relationship between habitus and disposition. The habitus is a system of dispositions, but is not the sum of these dispositions as such but rather their 'shared structure' (Hage 2013: 85). The shared structure of the soldier habitus is readiness; its 'durable way of standing, speaking, walking, and thereby of feeling and thinking' (Bourdieu 1990: 70) is the continual awareness of everything around you and the state of being poised to react. This enables soldiers to effectively snap into action if, for example, they are suddenly called up, run into enemy contact, detect signs of enemy movement on patrol, and so on. Soldiers call this alert, fully functional state being 'switched on', and it allows not only rapid response in the field but also focus during training.

What this means, then, is that doing something like leaving the barracks door unlocked is a sign that you have 'switched off' and you will be promptly told to 'switch on!' Part of the reason that the beds on Basic Training have to be perfectly made with not a hint of a wrinkle, and that pulling them apart is therefore an effective punishment, is that, as part of a general requirement that soldiers never slouch or slump, recruits cannot even sit on them during the day, as this potentially allows for recruits to 'switch off'. Likewise, you will be punished for leaning on the wall ('that wall's been standing for twenty years, it doesn't need your help') and only certain ways of sitting on open ground are acceptable: no lounging is allowed, and the only thing you can lean upon is one another's (upright) backs. Thus your body is always ready to react, and so is your mind; the lack of physical relaxation has prevented mental relaxation.

Four key soldiering dispositions

THE INCIDENT WITH THE DOOR therefore illustrates several soldier dispositions that all share the same underlying structure of readiness, in that they all contribute to soldiers' ability to embody the 'switched on' state. At Basic Training recruits were in the process of internalising these dispositions so that they would, eventually, become second nature. I will cover four of these dispositions, although there are more. These are not the four official army values I listed above, but rather more informal everyday dispositions, which I refer to here using slogans and sayings that training staff often invoked during Basic: *security*, *attention to detail*, *sense of urgency*, and *get over it*.

Security ensures the readiness of soldiers' equipment, and therefore the readiness of themselves; *attention to detail* is the way in which you become attuned to everything around you; *sense of urgency* enables you to react both quickly and effectively; and *get over it* produces mental and emotional readiness.

Because these dispositions are to be enacted in all areas of a soldier's life, whether in uniform or not, they are also taught through all areas of a recruit's life, and this is how the door and the beds become significant. This analysis, however, in no way had to be centred on a door. I could have started with almost any facet of daily life and ended up with the same analysis. This is because it's not just that you have to learn a small thing like remembering to shut and lock the bedroom door behind you; you have to learn dozens of such small things, and then perform them all simultaneously. The way that this works is that what are to become transposable dispositions are first introduced in their application to seemingly unimportant everyday things. Thus they may be learned not only in the field but also in the barracks and the mess.

Through the routines with which you accomplish basic daily tasks you learn skills that become embodied as dispositions, which can then be applied on deployment. Thus barracks routine is seen to build up to much more obviously martial skills. None of this was hidden from recruits, nor was it an obscure function that only an over-analytical anthropologist would uncover. Platoon staff always made sure to tell recruits the exact reason behind some meticulous requirement, and how it would help make them a good soldier, and they often reiterated that everything in the army came back to operations: 'You have to realise that all that stuff we do back in the barracks is applied out there too and does translate to the field.'

Once you have used soldier dispositions to 'square away' (tidy and organise) your living spaces and your belongings within them, these things become the visible proof that you have taken on these dispositions and are acting in line with them: that you pay attention to detail, move with a sense of urgency, and can switch on. If you have developed the skills to present yourself and your surroundings well and maintain these at all times under any circumstances, you have also developed soldier dispositions, and therefore will 'instinctively' act on these in training and in the field. With this in mind, I will now return to the case of the open door, and to the two reasons why my informants would never have told a researcher that leaving a door unlocked was a stupid thing for which to be punished: these are, firstly, that they saw this as a valid correction and therefore not a cause for complaint; and, secondly, that learning not to complain to outsiders is part of internalising the switched-on soldier habitus.

By leaving the bedroom door open, Miller and I showed that we had not internalised soldier dispositions. We couldn't unconsciously shut and lock it behind us, but still had to think to get it right, and did not even manage to do this thinking. Rather, we were still unconsciously acting on the civilian predispositions with which we had arrived, in which locking internal doors doesn't seem necessary. Examining the door incident in terms of the four dispositions of security, attention to detail, sense of urgency and get over it as measures of soldierhood clearly shows why we failed to live up to expectations.

Security

LOCKING THE DOOR IS A manifestation of the soldier disposition of *security*. The more obviously military functions of security are to always be aware of the whereabouts of your military kit, especially the very important items such as rifles and body armour, and to not let anything untoward happen to it, such as misplacing it, leaving it behind, or having it taken from you. Thus the field exercise version of the barracks focus on locking your door is that corporals will go crawling around in the middle of the night, seeing if there are any stray items lying around that they can pinch.

Everything should be squared away and present, whether this is in your wardrobe in your bedroom, or in your pack and webbing in the field. Soldiers are judged on whether their equipment is looking tidy and well-ordered. It is much harder to find something essential in a hurry on a field exercise or deployment if your pack is a mess. If your kit is ready to go, and you know exactly where every piece of it is, hence enabling you to grab anything the second you are called out, then you are ready to do your job, and are therefore a good soldier. If your kit isn't ready to go, if you have lost some of it because you have left your door open or your pack unsupervised, then you cannot react instantaneously and are not an effective soldier. The way in which the platoon commander chose to punish us thus demonstrates the disorder that can result if you don't always carefully consider the state of your belongings, but it also reveals other soldier dispositions.

Attention to detail and sense of urgency

THE ROOM NOW BEING IN such a mess was a big deal, because an inspection could be called at any time, and thus your bedroom needed to be as close as possible to a state of 'inspection order' at all times. Barracks inspections were constant and involved 'standing to beds' — standing at ease at the foot of your bed, with your wardrobe open and the rest of the bedroom and barracks spotless. Recruits folded their sheets and blankets into an intricate and symmetrical bundle called 'bedrolls' each morning. This consisted of three layers of blanket alternated with two layers of sheet, with a blanket wrapped around the whole bundle to contain it. These were then placed at the head of the bed, and topped with a pillow and then a folded pillowcase. The bed itself was covered by a blanket and counterpane. The blanket had a red line running down the middle which therefore had to be perfectly straight, and the counterpane was placed on top of this, pulled two-thirds of the way up the bed with perfect hospital corners. Yet now all of this formerly immaculate bedding was in heaps all over the floor. Like locking the door, these painstaking bed-making requirements were a way of inculcating soldier dispositions, this time the dispositions of attention to detail and sense of urgency. Hurricaning the room provided another opportunity to practise enacting these particular dispositions.

Attention to detail means being very aware of your surroundings, as well as being meticulous in everything that you do. Making the beds required paying close attention to details such as corners being perfectly square and lines being perfectly straight and parallel. It meant, for example, that if the fitted sheets weren't exactly the same shade of blue as the top sheets, you would coordinate with the rest of the platoon to make sure that you had all made the same decision about whether the darker or lighter sheet was in the higher layer of the bedroll. Attention to detail means being able to spot anything out of place, even if it's as small as a piece of fluff or a stray thread. This was applied outside of the barracks also. There were to be no leaves bigger than a 50-cent piece in the gardens, for example: 'Oh no, it's an apocalypse,' one recruit groaned when we stepped outside the morning after a strong wind. One of the more military applications of this disposition, of course, is being able to find even the smallest traces of enemy movement on patrol. If you unthinkingly pay close attention to the smallest details of your surroundings wherever you are, you are ready to spot anything that doesn't fit.

Meanwhile, the bedrolls and beds had to be made up rapidly each morning, in the midst of also showering and getting your uniform up to inspection standard. In this way recruits internalised *sense of urgency*, and learned that you can get quite a lot done in very small amounts of time (without of course forgetting attention to detail). Having to make bedrolls every morning therefore got you used to timings: 'I know some of you are thinking of sleeping in sleeping bags but cheating is only cheating yourself, if you get to your units and you can't get places on time.' Likewise, Miller and I now had to remake all of the beds rapidly, before the rest of the platoon finished cleaning the weapons and a barracks inspection could be called.

Once recruits have mastered some of the more onerous basic tasks, they get to move on from them, in recognition of their having taken on soldier dispositions: 'you guys are better than bedrolls now'. Bedrolls were eventually replaced with duvets. Making your bed with a duvet isn't easy, however, to the extent that some recruits wished they had stuck with the bedrolls. Your duvet has to end exactly 30 centimetres from the top of the bed, and anywhere that your duvet is creased has to be ironed. As the platoon stood around one of the bedrooms learning to iron their beds, the corporals explained the point of all this: the recruits were being taught to be pedantic with their kit, and to take care of their home. In the field your house is your pack, and the corporals noted especially that in the field you put something away as soon as you'd finished using it — everything neat and in its place.

A few days later the platoon was learning how to make a sangar (a temporary fortified position) out of sandbags. The sections were competing to construct the best corner. And indeed, the recruits were reminded of and drew on their bedmaking skills: squaring off layers, lining them up perfectly. 'This is like bedrolls!' one recruit declared. 'Make it tight.' And when we stopped for judging, another recruit jeered at an opposing section: 'You have creases! You haven't ironed your walls yet!'

In these ways, the army taught recruits that the small aspects of their everyday lives had a significant role to play in their attempts to transform themselves into soldiers. If they could make their beds perfectly and shut and lock their doors behind them, they could act securely, with attention to detail and with a sense of urgency, and could do so in the field as if by instinct without having to consciously think about it; the combination of all of these meant that they could switch on and were ready to immediately notice and deal with anything that might occur. Recruits adopted this viewpoint easily, not only because they were highly invested in the soldier identity, but also because this fitted the model of 'transformation through hardship' that they desired. They weren't, therefore, about to complain.

Get over it

THE RECRUITS WITH WHOM I was embedded at Basic would not, therefore, have characterised leaving the door insecure as a 'stupid thing' for which to be punished. When my informants later reflected on such punishments amongst themselves, once they had graduated as soldiers, they would treat them as funny stories and even treasured memories: 'At the time you're like, "this sucks", but afterwards you're like [mimes delighted hysterical laughter].' But even if they had thought this whole process was stupid, they would never have confessed this to a civilian, as Guesgen's informant did.

Had a soldier resented a punishment from their Basic Training, they might moan about it to their fellow recruits, but it would never go further than that. This is because of yet another soldier disposition that being hurricaned helps recruits internalise, which is to *get over it*. As a researcher, I was very lucky to hear the opinions that my informants would normally suppress around civilians. This was largely due to my having been present before and while the *get over it* disposition was internalised. This is one of the key ways in which participant observation works to generate insight: because you are around so much that you become familiar, people will stop reacting to you as an outsider and therefore stop adjusting their behaviour around you.

Getting over it is the ability to control one's emotions and opinions and not let them interfere with the job at hand, whatever that job is. The 'it' that must be got over is, eventually, everything and anything. However, recruits learned this disposition in a series of stages, with 'it' being a series of specific things emphasised at different times. In the early days of Basic Training, while we were being hurricaned for insecurity and other such infractions, the recruits were in the first stage of learning to get over it, and the 'it' was being reprimanded by staff. In the first month or two, staff would follow up every reprimand by telling us: 'Don't take it personally.' What they were trying to do was to teach the recruits to not get caught up in negative emotions when they were reprimanded — embarrassment, upset, resentfulness, or denial that you were wrong and needed to adjust. Dwelling on such emotions, at this stage of their army career, prevented recruits from taking criticism on board and improving. You had to be able to act on criticism immediately, and focus on the task at hand rather than wallow.

Thus the lesson of getting over it, as it is taught at Basic, is both a soldier disposition in itself *and* the process by which the other soldier dispositions, such as *attention to detail*, are taken on. In the long run, getting over it enabled the embodiment of readiness: it allowed you to not be distracted by your emotions when you needed to be switched on and focused solely on your present task, and to follow all orders and complete all tasks well despite your actual opinion of those orders or of who gave them.

Miller and I therefore simply couldn't grumble or sit around indulging in embarrassment for showing incompetence in front of the whole platoon, nor display guilt over the fact that all of the other girls' hard work had been undone by our own carelessness. Rather we had to immediately jump into getting all the beds back together. We had in fact not finished this task when the next round of punishments began. As we were making beds, everything suddenly went silent, indicating that Sir was now inspecting the weapons to make sure that all traces of carbon had been removed. The silence stretched on until behind the still-secure door we heard Sir begin to speak in a muffled voice and managed to catch the words 'wet weathers', and then the sounds of 30 people sprinting down the corridor, so we fetched the girls' wet weather gear out of the wardrobe for them to grab off us at the door.

Being punished often involves variants of 'change parades', which involve getting into and out of various uniforms and gear in rapid succession. This provides practice in getting ready quickly if you are called out, and also more generally helps internalise *sense of urgency*.

We spent the rest of the night being punished for a variety of faults: the platoon failed the weapons inspection (failure to display *attention to detail* in not finding and removing all traces of carbon, which could affect readiness if your rifle malfunctioned), and failed the barracks inspection when it was predictably called (failure to display *attention to detail* and *sense of urgency*). We were punished, too, for putting on the pretence of doubling with an exaggerated jog rather than actually doubling through the barracks (failure to display *sense of urgency*). Our punishments involved being given very small time periods to, for example, have our spare boots laced with the laces pulled tight and tucked away, have the soles of our running shoes immaculately clean, without a speck of dirt or gravel, have our green towels folded and placed over our laundry bag with the fold facing outwards, and so on (reinforcement of *sense of urgency* and *attention to detail*).

Amidst all of this activity, the only times when it was appropriate to remember that we had been hurricaned were whenever we next ran out the bedroom door — to prompt us to shut and lock it behind us — or at any other point when we needed to act on the disposition of *security*, until we were doing so as if by instinct, without needing to think about it at all. The other girls, meanwhile, demonstrated the soldier disposition of *get over it* (in this case, 'it' being our mistake affecting them) by not reproaching us for it. The only thing they ever said about the incident, in fact, was 'thank you for fixing the room'.

In a final comment on this matter, however, a few of my informants, months later and after Basic Training, once they felt that they had mastered the basics and were acting in line with the soldier dispositions, did start questioning whether simple everyday tasks really translated to more martial abilities. Barracks routine had been embraced at first because it was a challenge, but once recruits could remember to simultaneously have all their bedding parallel, all their laces tucked in and all their doors locked, these things became boring and they went looking for more challenges. By the time such questioning began to occur, however, my informants had already been trained to not let it affect their performance: unthinkingly acting in line with the *get over it* disposition, they would only make such comments to each other in down times. They would never dwell on them on the job, or air them publicly.

Conclusion

THE REASON I WAS SO surprised when I heard that Guesgen's informant saw not locking his door as a stupid thing to be punished for was that, to someone who has been present at a Basic Training, this is a sign that he had not taken on a soldier identity. It was not, of course, the case that everything I have covered in this chapter actually consciously ran through my head and resulted in my making this determination. Rather it was because through my own participation in barracks routines I had in fact partially internalised army dispositions myself. I instantly and unthinkingly reacted in line with them, the result being the visceral reaction of shock. Likewise, my own research informants' 'instinctive' reaction to being punished for mistakes such as leaving doors unlocked or not having perfect bedrolls was to work quickly to rectify the issue, and then immediately move on with no publicly visible lingering resentment.

The reason for the recruits both not seeing such a punishment as stupid and not recounting any dissatisfaction with their training to civilians are one and the same: they are both enactments of the same underlying soldier habitus, the ability to 'switch on'. Retaining indignation over an incident long enough for it to become one of the defining aspects of your military training (and hence worth discussing with a researcher) would interfere with the rest of this training process. Hence, even if you were inclined to react negatively at the time of the event, becoming a soldier meant you needed to learn to deal with such emotions.

To recruits, the fact that they had developed the ability to react to being hurricaned not by focusing on embarrassment or guilt or irritation but rather by putting all of these aside in order to not only get the room back together quickly but also use this as a learning experience, meant that their capabilities and their selves had been built up, not 'broken down'. Along with learning to remember to lock the door, this meant that the recruits had acquired new skills, and hence new dispositions, and were well on their way to embodying the soldier habitus. Acting on these new dispositions meant that later on in their military lives, even if they were punished for a reason they deemed to be stupid, or told to do something they perceived to be pointless, the new soldiers could complete that task effectively and even with apparent enthusiasm. They had, through their own hard work, embodied readiness and therefore the ability to deal with anything.

This, however, is only one point of view of the place of locks and doors in military training: the specific point of view of trainee soldiers during Basic Training. In the next chapter, Guesgen presents the point of view of her own informants, exploring the issue of barracks door security from the perspective of ex-officer cadets, who had internalised somewhat different dispositions.

A practice parade by the Royal New Zealand Medical Corps. All soldiers must undergo Basic Training before joining their corps.

02

Closing the Door on Military Life: The unmaking of officers

M. Guesgen

AFTER RETURNING FROM FIELDWORK WITH four officer cadets, I was discussing with my supervisor some of the stories my participants had told me about their time in the New Zealand Army. For one of the officer cadets, the challenge of meeting expectations at Linton Military Camp had begun to wear on him. 'Dawson' revealed that during his third year in the Kippenberger cadet programme he was being charged more frequently for what he called 'stupid things'. One of these 'stupid things' included leaving his door unlocked in barracks.

From the beginning of their training, 'Kipps' had been made aware of a written order stating that all doors were to be locked if an individual left their room unoccupied. When Dawson's door was found to be unlocked, and he was consequently charged for the offence, he remembers thinking:

> Oh my God, I've got to get out of this . . . it was like I'd left school where at least I was kind of treated like an adult, and then to come back as being just the shittiest little shit Kipp at the bottom of the heap . . . that's what it felt like to me. And they just totally had complete control over your life . . . I just didn't feel like there was any mutual respect.

When my supervisor mentioned this incident to my colleague, Harding, however, she was shocked to hear that an event such as leaving a door unlocked had occurred and, furthermore, that my participant had *complained* about being charged.

For my research project I had originally interviewed a number of former members of the Kippenberger scheme in an attempt to understand why certain individuals had not made it as officers in the New Zealand Army. This chapter focuses on one particular member in order to track his journey in a more detailed way, the better to understand the circumstances leading up to the 'incident with the door'. Dawson left the army before becoming a commissioned officer. Using the concept of the neoliberalist generation to help explain his experiences, I will explore why the indoctrination into the military was not successful for him, and what we can potentially learn about the *unmaking* of officers in the New Zealand Army.

In terms of how I explore this topic, this chapter engages in narrative analysis, a form of analysis that is qualitative in nature. That is, this type of research involves analysing the meaning of verbal and written accounts of the social world to produce a descriptive interpretation of collected data (Gilbert 2008). Qualitative research is characterised by its holistic approach to a subject, which focuses on the interrelated elements that make up the individual's experience (Vuga and Juvan 2013: 118). As Gilbert states, this type of approach makes it less problematic to 'follow cause and effect' (35) in the individual's description of a particular event, as the data is not reduced to numbers (Carreiras and Alexandre 2013). This was important because Dawson's story included topics on his childhood, family and friends, and his personal interests and world view, amongst other things. During the interview I may have found a particular part of the discussion to be disjointed, but when I reviewed my transcript, I began to see relationships and connections form. Information from my participant can therefore be tracked, analysed and understood through his description; thus this chapter continues the anthropological approach adopted earlier by Harding.

The Kippenberger scheme

A BRIEF REVIEW OF THE Kippenberger scheme explains the circumstances under which Dawson spent his time in the New Zealand Army. The scheme, named after former Major General Sir Howard Kippenberger, was founded by the army in 1995 to provide officer cadets with a tertiary education from Massey University, Palmerston North, prior to commissioning (Forde 1998: 1; Wheeler 2011: 1). The scheme (which ran until 2011) provided this education at no cost to its participants, thus removing the financial burden from parents who might otherwise have expected to help fund their children through university.

Although there is not much in the way of public information from the New Zealand Defence Force (NZDF) on why the army should have wanted officers with a tertiary education, one of my interviewees offered an explanation. He believed that the army was seeking both to increase intelligence and knowledge levels amongst officers and to entice young people to join the military: 'The Kipp scheme came along and it was like, hey we [the army] can give you a degree, we'll pay for it, as long as you join the military.'

To qualify for the programme, the individuals I interviewed were required to apply to the Officer Selection Board, and were sent to a five-day officer's selection at Trentham Military Camp (NZDF 2014). Here, the applicants were grouped into syndicates of approximately six individuals and tested on their physical and psychological abilities, as well as their capacity to work as part of a team. At the conclusion of the five days, applicants were informed as to whether or not they had been accepted into the officer training programme. Those selected were sent to Waiouru Military Camp for seven weeks to complete Initial Officer Training (IOT).

IOT, which has since been replaced by the Joint Officer Induction Course (JOIC), familiarised recruits with basic military skills, including 'field-craft, weapon handling, navigation, drill, battle-craft, communications, and an introduction to leadership' (NZ Defence Careers 2013b: 4). At the conclusion of their IOT, officer cadets possessed the same skill set that soldiers had gained during their Basic Training, but then the skill sets diverged. Following IOT, the officer cadets began university studies.

Stationed initially in Palmerston North from a civilian base, and later transferred to Linton Military Camp in 2001, my Kippenberger interviewees worked towards completing their degree of choice at Massey University. Spending the majority of their time studying towards their degree, the officer cadets also attended physical training sessions, inspections and parades during weekdays, as well as exercises held on weekends across the North Island. During the university semester officer cadets were required to maintain a B-grade average in all their subjects, which included assignment marks, in-class tests and the final exam at the end of each semester. If successful in maintaining this average while also meeting their military training obligations, the officer cadets were then sent back to Waiouru Military Camp after finishing university study to commence their army officer training at the New Zealand Commissioning Course (NZCC).

Building on the knowledge that the officer cadets learned during their IOT, the NZCC was the last phase of training for Kipps before taking an army commission. The course, spanning a year, aimed to create officers who were capable of leading soldiers for both New Zealand and overseas tasks (NZ Defence Careers 2013b). The participants of the Kippenberger scheme therefore gained both a tertiary education and a commission into the New Zealand Army as army officers.

The primary role of an army officer is to be a leader (ibid.). The Kipps call on decision-making and problem-solving skills learned during their NZCC year to lead and inspire their soldiers through challenging and often demanding situations. Following this year, each officer joins a corps specialising in one of the following trades: combat, specialist, engineering and technical trades, medical and health, intelligence and communications, hospitality, or logistics and administration. Within each trade there is a combination of officers and soldiers; it is expected that officers will lead, direct and organise soldiers on the ways in which tasks are to be completed. Each trade has a specific function contributing towards the overall working of the New Zealand Army.

Understanding the aims and processes of the Kippenberger scheme provides part of the context for understanding Dawson's experiences, but it helps, too, to understand the overall societal context of the time: in particular, the influence of neoliberalism.

The neoliberal generation

YOUNG NEW ZEALANDERS BORN IN the years following 1984 are considered to be the country's 'neoliberal generation'. It was from that year on that major economic and social policy reforms initially undertaken by the Third Labour Government transformed New Zealand's economy and society. Amongst other things, the restructurings of the 1980s produced significant inequality, which was magnified in the 1990s by further social reforms. Following a recommendation by the Treasury, the subsequent Fourth National Government cut welfare benefits in an attempt to reduce inflation and unemployment levels (Nairn et al. 2012: 14).

One of the flow-on effects of all of these reforms was the development of the tertiary education sector, with state policy emphasising the goal that 'every young person should be in education, training or employment' (ibid: 16). From the early 1990s, student participation at universities and polytechnic institutes rose (Pollock 2012: 1), and universities became more entrepreneurial in marketing themselves, given that funding was based on the number of students in attendance (Nairn et al. 2012: 15). The introduction of student loans aimed to eliminate financial barriers to tertiary education for youth, in order to create a competitive environment amongst these education providers (ibid.: 48). Student fees, targeted allowances and stricter criteria for welfare eligibility all contributed to the expectation that parents would subsidise their children's education and training (Nairn et al. 2012: 16). Because of these developments in tertiary education, the youth labour market collapsed. This transformed what used to be the standard pathways out of school, where youth would enter the workforce straight away. For school leavers facing intense competition from experienced labour in the workplace, post-school education became an obvious next step.

Members of the neoliberal generation have therefore faced unprecedented changes to traditional life-course patterns. They are likely to move between education and employment on a continual basis, not expecting to settle into a single job over their lifetime (ibid.: 17). They are likely to move in and out of the family home, to have meaningful relationships comparatively early on, and to set out relatively late in young adulthood to buy their first home. This unique set of properties indicates that these individuals are responsible for making their own choices about their lives, and contributes to the construction of their identity.

Nairn et al. (2012) suggest that for the neoliberal generation, constructing an identity is carried out in the enactment and performance of that identity, which is 're-created during social, cultural and physical activities' (89). We might extend this to say that young people within the neoliberal generation can either *embrace or renounce* a particular identity through social interactions. By placing Dawson's narrative in the context of the neoliberal generation we may be better able to understand why he did not lock the door behind him. To begin with, however, it is important to understand how he came to be involved in the Kippenberger scheme in the first place.

Joining the military

FOR DAWSON, BROUGHT UP WITHIN a military family, participation in a military institution seemed like an obvious career choice. However, although in his interview he draws on his father's experience, he refers to his own move as a stepping stone in his transition from high school into full-time employment, stating that his father did not force him to pursue a certain career, but rather that 'he sort of saw I didn't really know what I wanted to do per se, so he was just like, well this is what I know so why don't you go this way . . . at least you're going forwards'. The suggestion of serving in the military also fitted nicely with Dawson's desire to help others. Dawson had already established certain views of the military based on what his father had experienced, but this view was soon to be challenged.

Having opted to take part in the Kippenberger scheme, Dawson underwent the five-day officer's selection at Trentham. According to another Kipp, of the total number applying for IOT only 5 per cent had been selected to become commissioned officers. And of this 5 per cent, only a third made it into the Kippenberger scheme, with 12 individuals being selected in the year that Dawson joined. After passing officer selection, Dawson transferred to Waiouru to complete IOT.

The reality of IOT came as a shock to Dawson. 'I'd only seen the top parts and this was right at the bottom. You're lower than dirt. That's what disillusioned it [*sic*] for me at the start.' As a result, he pushed against the rules and regulations of the army at an early stage in his officer training. During his time at Waiouru, Dawson felt that he was being treated as a criminal:

> The rules are so harsh that the only way you can actually get things done is by taking short cuts; and so, inadvertently, they're telling you on the one hand that you have to follow all the rules and procedures, and on the other they're telling you that you need to take short cuts to get through it.

It can be seen from Dawson's description of IOT that he came in with distinctly different ideas of military training compared with those of

Harding's soldiers (see previous chapter). Military training, as he saw it, was the army attempting to break him down, and something that he would not stand for as it did not meet his expectations of what army life was supposed to be: 'easy'.

Army–student life

AFTER SIX WEEKS OF TRAINING at Waiouru Military Camp, the officer cadets of the Kippenberger scheme graduated from IOT. They were now ready to be moved to Linton Military Camp in Palmerston North, where they would commence their studies at Massey University. After completing IOT, Dawson found initially that Palmerston North was a welcome change, with new-found freedoms. He enjoyed

> . . . being able to chill, have beers on the roof, just be students. Because we were students as well. We were soldiers and we'd just done hardcore soldiering for six weeks, and now it's O week[1] and we want to be students, we're allowed to be students in that first year.

But as Dawson settled into life at Linton, the disillusionment grew: the lived reality of the Kippenberger programme did not match his original expectations. This led him to rebel, resulting in incidents such as leaving a door unlocked. This recalls the assertion by Nairn et al. (2012) that, for the neoliberal generation, crafting an identity is carried out through the performance of that identity. When he was not able to meet the requirements set out by the army, Dawson was inhibited from enacting an identity for himself that fitted with what the army sought to create: officers that had a tertiary education along with the values and ethos of the New Zealand Army.

---

1. 'O week' refers to orientation week, the period of familiarisation and socialising at university before studies begin.

In terms of his university experience, Dawson chose to complete a Bachelor of Arts with a major in Defence Studies, which pleased him as he was able to see the relationship between university study and military training. He states, however, that it was not just the army–university balance that he had to uphold, but also a social aspect to his life. Dawson remembers having difficulty in maintaining these three aspects, especially when training became more frequent outside regular weekday hours. He did not see the other officer cadets *as* his social life, and this reveals a disconnect: had he regarded his social life as something that involved his peers, it might have influenced him to take the values and ethos of the army more seriously.

In his efforts to balance military and university demands, Dawson managed to do an adequate amount of study towards his degree, but he remembers reaching a point where he could no longer sustain his commitment to the army. 'The only way you could really justify it was that you knew you'd get a full-time job out of it at the end, and be an officer. But then I started thinking, "I don't want to be an officer or in the army."' Dawson's third year saw him being charged more frequently, for — in his view — minor offences. The turning point came when he was confined to camp for a significant period of time (later discussions indicated that this period was longer than usual, which perhaps suggests other tensions at work) due to the 'incident with the door'.

Dawson was charged with disobeying a written order stating that an officer cadet's door should be locked at all times within barracks. In his view, the officers disciplining the officer cadets upheld the notion that 'military discipline needs to be applied at all times', and they did not understand what it was like to be on the receiving end of a charge. He believes he should have been treated according to the conventions by which 'soldiers fit into normal society'. He found their actions 'totally unnecessary, and at the moment they're struggling to retain numbers, so I wonder why they're not treating their employees that well'. However, it was that very same 'normal society' that contributed to Dawson's failure to fully take on officer training.

Post-Kippenberger

THE KIPPENBERGER SCHEME WAS CANCELLED at the end of 2011 after the army recognised that it was failing to 'install the requisite Army Culture' (Wheeler 2011: 1) in the officer cadets of the programme and as the NZDF faced pressure to cut costs. This required Dawson, who was still part of the scheme at the time, to reconsider his future plans. Interestingly, this decision was almost a non-event for Dawson because he had already expected such action to be taken by the army. One of the other participants of the Kippenberger scheme also recollected that he 'kind of knew it was coming'. Indeed, after Dawson received a string of warnings from the army, and failed to attend examinations at Massey University, his course of action was selected for him when he was dismissed from the Kippenberger scheme before the programme officially ceased.

After leaving the army, Dawson attempted to complete the remaining year of his degree while also maintaining full-time work, but struggled to balance the two obligations. A turning point came when he realised he wanted to be a teacher. As noted above, one of Dawson's incentives for joining the military was that he wanted to be deployed in order to help others; he now found that teaching would provide the same opportunity.

Reflecting on his experiences in the Kippenberger scheme, Dawson suggested that he and potentially also his fellow cadets did not fit in during his time at Linton, and therefore he found it difficult to take written orders seriously. Because the programme focused on training officer cadets, Dawson remembers being treated as an outsider by other military personnel at the training camp. There were, he states,

> the officers and the soldiers, and we were in between because we

> were officer cadets, but we were actually technically below the other ranks. But we were about to make a significant leap to be on top of all the other ranks as officers. . . . we were sort of just isolated in the middle, not allowed to interact with the officers or other ranks.

This, coupled with the impression of not having control over his life, made him reluctant to follow written orders and regulations as some of his other colleagues were able to do. Moreover, having to be the one to give orders was another factor contributing to his departure; he found that if he had to give an order with which he didn't agree and which would negatively affect his men he 'wouldn't be able to do it'. Since embarking on a career as a secondary school teacher, Dawson has had a number of revelations that have changed his perception of the individual he wants to be. He found that the army 'didn't fit who I was any more . . . I think I just grew up, and not in the way the army wanted me to'.

Conclusion

IT CAN BE SEEN, THEN, that Dawson's narrative centred largely on a feeling of disillusionment. His unrest, and therefore his lack of commitment, resulted at least in part from belonging to a generation with particular characteristics. He saw himself as an employee of the military, rather than in its service. Thus he could not fully identify with being a Kippenberger, an identity that encompasses both the academic side — which includes university participation to a high standard, meeting grades and attending classes — and the military side, which incorporated the ethos, values and behaviours the New Zealand Army wanted to instil in all its military personnel. Had both of these sides to the Kippenberger identity been present in Dawson, he would have successfully locked his door behind him, as he would have fully adopted the ethos and values established by the army during IOT. Moreover, even if he had forgotten this task, had he internalised army values properly he would have accepted and even welcomed the charge that followed. The fact that he did neither implies that, for my interviewee, one part of his identity had given way to the other.

Recalling again the comments of Nairn et al. (2012) on the crafting of identities, it can be said that Dawson felt as though his identity was unable to develop into the model the army wanted. What this potentially demonstrates is that young people of the neoliberal generation feel entitled to either embrace or renounce a particular identity. Attempting to perform that identity, to see whether or not it fits, is what allows young people to test whether a particular identity works for them.

Through the setbacks with the army, my interviewee developed a sense of what he wanted to associate with, and therefore how he wanted to identify himself. Because the army was not what Dawson wanted for himself, it can be understood why he chose to disregard a written order. Identity is produced through an individual's own contemplation of their personal biography, which is a product of the individual's reflexive understandings of their own life. This is why 'the incident of the door' occurred.

The Kippenberger scheme was named after Major General Sir Howard Kippenberger. He served for two months at the Western Front in the First World War, before being sent home wounded, and went on to become Commander of the New Zealand Division in the Second World War. He is pictured here (left) with Charles Upham in Egypt in 1941. REF: DA-02149-F. ALEXANDER TURNBULL LIBRARY.

03

Reconsidering Military Identities: Professional Anzacs doing development?

Samantha Morris

THE PREVIOUS TWO CHAPTERS CONSIDERED how military identity may be created or rejected. We now consider how military identity is challenged, reinforced or remade by engagement in tasks that have not traditionally been core military activities. Like the preceding work, this chapter draws on discussions with NZDF personnel. In this case, though, it draws on a slightly different method of engagement and accesses sociological concepts to help analyse the findings and ideas raised. Semi-structured interviews (where fairly open-ended questions are asked) with 10 personnel who had served with the New Zealand Provincial Reconstruction Team (NZ PRT) in Afghanistan provide the information to help round out a picture of a possible 'New Zealand military identity'.

The deployment of military units in insecure environments with broadly non-war-fighting objectives has been the source of much debate in both academic and practitioner literatures. These non-war-fighting objectives, in many instances, involve some combination of humanitarian intervention, post-conflict reconstruction, governance reform and development: areas that are arguably the concern of civilian actors. At a theoretical or macro-political level the expansion of the military into these areas is, for some scholars (such as Duffield 2005; Ignatieff 2003), symptomatic of a pervasive trend of what is called 'securitisation'. At the operational level in these types of environment, as others in this volume such as Fish et al. will also note, the line between the civilian actor and the soldier is blurred. Moreover, some of the roles undertaken by military forces may arguably be incompatible with both the organisational culture of militaries and the identity of personnel. This chapter examines one relevant example of involvement by the New Zealand Defence Force (NZDF) in post-2001 Afghanistan. It considers the experiences of personnel who served with the NZ PRT in Bamiyan province during 2003–13 and explores issues arising from military engagement in non-war-fighting tasks.

Examining the PRT itself presents an interesting model of civil–military engagement in insecure environments. PRTs were designed to address the recognition that a degree of support for civilian populations was missing in Afghanistan 'between the immediate tactical application of military activity and the eventual concerted international community development effort' (Pruett 2009: 56). Tasked with guaranteeing security in specific provinces while facilitating reconstruction and development, PRTs occupied a different space to military units deployed solely to alleviate humanitarian crises. Investigating the workings of the PRT provides an insight into the types of roles, tasks and functions that militaries are increasingly asked to undertake; meanwhile, examining the experiences of individual personnel who served on these PRTs helps us to better understand how such deployments might influence the way military personnel position themselves in this context — that is, how these changing roles might have an impact on military identity.

More precisely, this chapter investigates how experiences with development practice can both reify (make more concrete) and challenge conceptions of military identity. The first section sets a broader theoretical context for this discussion before moving on to an overview of the formation and operational details of the NZ PRT. Following this, the second section discusses identity in the context of the NZDF, considering two possible identities NZDF personnel may draw on when relating their experiences with development work in Afghanistan. These two identities draw on 1) the historical–cultural narrative of the Anzac soldier as well as 2) a more modern discourse of military professionalism. While the Anzac identity in particular remains important for personnel in understanding what constitutes a 'New Zealand way of doing things', its status as a 'force multiplier' may be limited by the absence of fully realised structures needed for supporting development work. The question of whether military personnel *should* be undertaking development or other key traditionally non-military tasks is discussed in more detail later in this volume.

Background

IN THE LITERATURE ON MILITARY involvement in humanitarian or development tasks the civilian is often positioned as the soldier's antithesis rather than a potential ally. At the theoretical level, when security problems are addressed by security institutions only and development problems are addressed by development institutions only the battlefield ceases to be seen for what it is — a space historically shared by civilian and military personnel (Ankersen 2008; Sannerholm 2013). The discussion over what roles should be played by whom is rife with disagreement. Some see militaries working to improve livelihoods while eliminating the spoilers of peace as a best-of-both-worlds scenario; others argue that this is deeply unethical. Many have questioned whether military personnel are capable of undertaking humanitarian and development activities, due to differences in civilian and military organisational cultures, expertise and priorities (Winslow 2005; Egnell 2008: 415; Fish et al., this volume).

Others, however, assert that the arguments of Winslow and others are based in an understanding of the military as a monolithic entity. Rubinstein (2012) reflected on his research with peacekeepers in Egypt as follows:

> One of the things that struck me . . . was that many . . . would frequently talk about people and organisations of the national security state in ways that they would never speak about other peoples or institutions. I observed, for instance, that our anthropological community would sharply condemn sweeping statements about 'The Arabs' as essentialising and totalising, appropriately noting that among these peoples and communities there was considerable variation; however, our anthropological community rarely challenged those who routinely spoke of 'The Military' as though no such variation exists. Yet, militaries are as varied and complex as other human communities. (193)

Moreover, as another academic has noted, 'arguments founded on a belief that all militaries are bad (due to their use of force) and all humanitarians are good (due to the nature of their moral motivations) cannot advance our understanding of real-world practices' (Ankersen 2008: 2).

The research that forms the foundation of this chapter therefore aims to do what Ankersen suggests by examining an example of this debate over military involvement in traditionally non-military tasks in practice; namely, it examines an instance where military personnel were expected both to do humanitarian or development work and to act as security guarantors.

The PRT

FOLLOWING THE TOPPLING OF THE Taliban regime in Afghanistan in late 2001, coalition forces, while having addressed the immediate humanitarian crisis, were criticised for failing to recognise the importance of the post-Taliban reconstruction phase (Ansary 2014; McNerney 2008). Provincial Reconstruction Teams were proposed and formed by the United States Armed Forces to bridge this gap; their role focused on 'strengthening all three pillars of security, governance and economic development with the emphasis shifting to enabling greater [reconstruction] and [development] as a province stabilizes and becomes more development-permissive' (ISAF 2009: 7).

The high profile afforded by contributing to a PRT made it a favoured option in New Zealand, and the option of taking over the Bamiyan PRT in particular was an attractive one for a number of reasons. Arms and narcotics trafficking was fairly low-level, the province had relatively minor infrastructure damage following the conflict, and a supportive provincial administration was already in situ (New Zealand Aid Programme [NZAP] 2013). In what was described as a turnkey operation, due to the ease of transferring the base over to New Zealand hands, New Zealand arranged to continue receiving logistical support from the US airbase at Bagram, and the handover of the base itself occurred on 23 September 2003 (Hoadley 2011).

Planned as a joint military operation — that is, involving all three services of the NZDF — the NZ PRT task group known as 'CRIB' was commanded by a field-grade colonel or equivalent from 2003 to 2010 (Hoadley 2011). With initial staffing at around 100 personnel, the number increased over time to 140, in addition to support personnel working in both Bagram and Kabul (NZ Cabinet External Relations and Defence Committee 2013; Hoadley 2011; ibid. 2015). Deployments were typically rotated approximately every six months, with the command team travelling to Bamiyan ahead of time to begin the handover process (Hoadley 2015). The majority of the 140 personnel were stationed at Kiwi Base, which was situated just outside of Bamiyan town in the north-east of the province. The NZ PRT engaged in extensive patrolling of the province and maintained two Forward Operating Bases (FOBs): Romero in Khamard District, and Chunuk Bair in Yakawalang District (Hall 2010). Each FOB was staffed by a patrol of 12, led by a commanding officer; other team members included infantry personnel and a medic, driver, and signals officer, in addition to a liaison officer (LO), who was responsible for engaging with communities, district governors and administrators (with assistance from patrol commanders) in order to coordinate security, reconstruction and development activities. Patrols often travelled beyond their FOBs to isolated parts of the province (ibid.).

While the emphasis placed on their role as facilitators of development and reconstruction fluctuated over time in concert with the character of the security environment, funding for development projects increased over the period of the deployment (NZAP 2013). The PRT development group acted as the hub for PRT-facilitated development projects, managing priorities communicated to patrols by communities in addition to those identified by provincial and district government bodies (Hall 2010). While facilitated by the PRT, projects and programmes were approved based on available funding as well as their coherence with the Afghan National Development Strategy (ANDS) and the Bamiyan Provincial Development Plan (PDP), and with the priority areas identified by the New Zealand government. These areas were education, governance, justice and the rule of law, health, humanitarian assistance and reconstruction (managed primarily by the NZDF), and sustainable economic development (including agriculture, renewable energy and tourism) (NZAP 2013).

From 2003 to 2005 development assistance was delivered primarily through NZDF channels before the establishment of an Afghanistan Programme within the New Zealand Aid Programme in 2005, at which point available funding increased (ibid.). Over time the priorities of the PRT became more development-oriented, culminating in the transition to MFAT (Ministry of Foreign Affairs and Trade) lead in 2010 with the appointment of Dick Newlands as PRT director (Taylor-Doig 2013). As of the 2012/13 financial year NZ$80.63 million was spent on development in Afghanistan by the New Zealand government, with a substantial increase in funding committed in the year prior to the withdrawal of the PRT (NZAP 2013). New Zealand's expenditure in Afghanistan in the period 2006–12 ranged between NZ$5 million and NZ$10 million. In the 2012/13 financial year this increased to nearly NZ$25 million (MFAT 2014; NZAP 2013: 5). Significantly, in addition to MFAT funding, the PRT was able to access the contestable Commander's Emergency Response Programme (CERP) fund managed by the US which, while largely infrastructure-oriented, was the largest source of development funding for the PRT in 2008 at over US$20 million (Hoadley 2011).

In beginning to segue into a discussion as to what this all meant, the experiences of individual military personnel undertaking development work in this context showed that they understood both their security and their development responsibilities in a number of different ways. Security, for them, was not solely confined to threats and responses to those threats, but also included the sense or feeling of security that their presence in the province brought. Development, too, as Cowen and Shenton (1996: 4) argue, was 'defined in a multiplicity of ways', not solely as the undertaking or result of projects or programmes but also as the act of engaging with the population, building relationships and trust through communication. These multiple understandings disrupt the causal links and linear timelines that are often drawn between the creation of a secure space and the subsequent success of development — instead suggesting that at times these processes are one and the same.

Further, the experiences that personnel had with development in practice were similar in many ways to reflections of civilian development practitioners operating in similar environments. This is significant, as it undermines assertions that the military is a monolithic institution whose structures are fundamentally incompatible with non-war-fighting development activities. The degree to which personnel reflected critically on development, and how this reflection encouraged them to adjust their practice, suggests that reflexivity and culturally sensitive practice are by no means the exclusive property of the civilian development community.

A New Zealand military identity?

IN THE REFLECTIONS OF PERSONNEL who participated in this research, the concept of identity surfaced again and again as an explanatory tool for their conduct in facilitating development projects and programmes. As already intimated in the preceding chapters, reflecting on identity opens up a broader discussion around 'how our concepts of ourselves affect our daily lives', and the means by which different identities are understood, performed and reproduced (Liu, McCreanor, McIntosh and Teaiwa 2005: 13). In the sociological literature (as related to the anthropological point of view expressed in the previous two chapters) this exercise is captured in the concept of 'identity work', which is concerned with examining the 'distinction between people's "internal" self-identities and the "external" social identities to which they relate' (Watson 2008: 123). Conceptualisations of an individual's identity as unchanging or essential are also challenged by the idea that self-identity is dynamic and constantly reshaped by competing discourses and practices (Watson 2008). Perhaps most relevant for this chapter is the notion that consideration of self-identity is exceptionally important with respect to helping to better understand how collectively constituted professional and national identities influence the actions of individuals (Higate and Cameron 2006; 2011).

In thinking about self-identity and its relationship to collective professional and national identity, NZDF personnel drew on two distinguishable identity discourses in relating their experiences of development work in Afghanistan. The first, an easily recognisable discourse to many New Zealanders, was the Anzac identity; the second was a more contemporary understanding of professionalism and professional identity.

The Anzac identity

THE 'ANZAC DISCOURSE' IS A compelling example of a representation of New Zealand-military identity, having emerged as a collective myth following the First World War and retrospectively applied to earlier military deployments. Harding (2008: 41) makes note of the most common characteristics of the Anzac identity as 'military prowess or superiority, self-control, egalitarianism, mateship, ingenuity and larrikinism'. These are all traits, historians and others have suggested, that were constitutive of New Zealand civilian-male identity *before* being canonised by the experiences of WWI (King 2003; Hucker 2010).

A belief in military prowess situates the New Zealander as a 'natural soldier' (McLeod 1986), who was 'endowed with more raw physical and military potential than the British regular' (Bennett 2003: 24) and who, in the face of danger and the absence of proper training, would still display stoicism and inner discipline (or self-control). Egalitarian in their approach to relationships with commanding officers, as well as across races, classes and genders, Anzacs displayed fairness and disliked authority. 'Presented as gifted amateurs who can fix technical problems, find substitutes for something unavailable, or find a better or easier way to carry out a task', ingenuity too is central (Harding 2008: 48). Larrikinism, the final component, draws on the stereotype of the 'lad' who goes to war in search of adventure.

While peacekeeping, contemporary warfare, development and reconstruction are all far removed from the experiences of WWI Anzacs, continued evocation of this identity is evident in the memorialisation of those soldiers who lost their lives in Afghanistan by New Zealand Governor-General Sir Jerry Mateparae, who emphasised that '[t]hey continue a proud tradition. A tradition of ordinary men and women who stepped forward to serve a higher calling' (as quoted by Taylor-Doig 2013: 5). The reference to 'ordinary men and women' draws on the foundational characteristic of the Anzac identity, which establishes the position of a New Zealand soldier as an 'everyman', a civilian with little or no training, who draws on their civilian skills to emerge militarily superior to soldiers of other nationalities (Harding 2008; King 2003). Positioning the 'everyman' as exceptional is common in the Anzac discourse, with stories of low-ranking soldiers stepping up to positions of authority plentiful, as are examples of senior officers ceding authority or readily taking advice from those of a lower rank (Donald 2005; Harding 2008). The addition that Mateparae makes of 'ordinary . . . women' suggests that while not a feature of the historical discourse, the role of gender in the NZDF's perception of itself and the New Zealand soldier has changed over time.

In their approach to development practice, personnel reproduced this Anzac discourse by situating themselves and their team members as ordinary and their approach as natural or unexceptional, simply solving problems in 'the old Kiwi way', as one research participant remarked. The Kiwi way consisted of a focus on interpersonal skills, with personnel describing themselves and their peers as respectful (particularly of other cultures), polite, honest, genuine, trusting and humble. This discourse was most evident in the reflections of some of the more senior personnel, for instance:

> Whether you're military or not, we tend to come across as more friendly, more engaged, more interested . . . The example I would use is where if we came to a village we would slow down, and if we did stop you know we'd find a couple of people and talk to the senior folk. There'd obviously be a couple of guys standing around sort of doing the security thing but there'd be another couple of guys who'd be a block down the road kicking a football around with some kids. Whereas you'd get an American team coming through you know if they're going through a village they wouldn't slow down, they'd be going straight through; if they did stop they'd be standing around looking pretty armed up, you know, [with] sunglasses and helmets — yeah, looking quite threatening. I think we were less threatening, and, um, more open to engaging;

> and that's not just Afghanistan, that's everywhere we go, yeah. And there's a difference between us and the Australians in that respect: Australians aren't as hard-out; well they're somewhere in between [New Zealand and the US] . . . and many people are aware of this and ask about it and try and do studies on it but it's very, very difficult to say why it is the case and I think it's just how we're brought up.

The suggestion that NZDF personnel, particularly those of a lower rank, possess an innate ability to be exceptional in a development context was attributed not to training but to their natural way of acting, their ordinariness. Egalitarianism, too, featured strongly, with personnel reflecting on New Zealanders as respectful, open and understanding. Multiculturalism and particularly the emphasis placed on Māori culture (Hohaia 2016) were foregrounded, with the NZDF seen as 'lucky' by most of the participants to be diverse in its ethnic make-up (as of 2012, Māori made up over 17.4 per cent of the total regular force of the NZDF [Rolfe 2015], but they have been historically under-represented in the officer classes [Scoppio 2010]). An internal culture of respect and openness was linked to an enhanced ability to operate in a development context (particularly post-conflict), noting the power of external military forces to display acceptance of difference and fairness in their interactions with civilians, challenging stereotypes and leading by example. One research participant spoke on this subject:

> I think it's ingrained in us from the day we enlist to respect culture, and we're lucky in New Zealand where we've got the combination of two cultures that are combined, whether you're of European ancestry or Māori; and we actually respect other [people's] cultures through that, so we've got a better understanding [of] and affinity with other cultures — especially indigenous people, you know

> — compared with other countries. And that sort of thing . . . is a sort of force multiplier, being able to get on with the locals and everything else, and when you look back over history, or recent history through the Asia-Pacific, [and] the sort of conflicts that we've been involved with, New Zealand soldiers stood out in those. In the jungles of Malaya, Borneo, Thailand, Vietnam, you know, working and living with locals, you know, it's probably almost second nature for us. Yeah: we're quite resilient, you know, and we're quite used to living in hardy conditions . . .

The necessity of exercising ingenuity, in this context, presumed the absence of sufficient means by which to achieve a set goal, or the application of one's skills to achieve outcomes beyond those set goals. In development facilitation this involved moving beyond organisational directives and responding creatively when faced with a development problem in order to maximise impact for local communities. Some personnel attributed ingenuity in development processes to the outcome-oriented mind-set that militaries instil in their soldiers.

These reflections also positioned personnel as in solidarity with, and accountable to, the population of Bamiyan. Harding (2008: 67) has noted that this sense of responsibility 'to make a meaningful contribution in the world despite the country's size and isolation' is common in many explanations of New Zealand military or diplomatic action. As one participant commented, 'the New Zealand way of doing things [meant] all hands to the pump', making the most of available resources and employing ingenuity to 'get on to it' in solving problems as they presented themselves. Another participant concurred on this point, suggesting that 'I think what we've always employed in the NZDF is a get on with it mentality. The "yep we acknowledge there's a gap here but we'll get on with it and do the best job we can" . . . it relies a lot on the personality and the capabilities of the individual.' This sentiment reflects the soldiering qualities of 'get over it' emphasised by Harding in this volume, and brings us to the notion of professionalism.

The professional identity

WHILE THE ANZAC CIVILIAN–SOLDIER DISCOURSE remains salient, this identity is increasingly being challenged in discussions of contemporary New Zealand-military identity. The development of the NZDF from a principally civilian expeditionary force during the first and second world wars to a professional force staffed by career servicemen and -women is suggested to have been a principal catalyst in this shift in identity. In her earlier work, Harding (2008) noted the presence of a 'career discourse' amongst 40 Squadron personnel where, for some, their role in support of the Gulf War was spoken about as an aspect of their career development, a job rather than a duty or service to their country. Similar emphases on this being a particular form of 'employment' occur in Guesgen's work in this volume. Additionally, the gradual redefinition of the NZDF soldier from a martial warrior prepared for total war to a peacekeeper brings into question the utility of the Anzac discourse.

While a focus is often placed on the process by which humanitarian and development assistance is politicised or militarised by the increased involvement of military units in such assistance, Forster (2006) has argued that there exists a parallel process whereby the military is 'humanitarianised' or 'civilianised' to serve changing interests in the domestic and international realms. Such changes could constitute a challenge to conventional constructions of military identity. However, for New Zealand, as Mayell (2004) argues, accepting that our security has always been vested collectively has resulted in a necessary examination of the capabilities of its armed forces against their operational responsibilities, namely stabilisation and peacekeeping operations. In this context, military personnel have found succour in a different form of identity.

Professionalism has been elevated as a tool of 'identity assemblage' (Higate 2011). What constitutes professional behaviour in the context of a given armed force depends greatly on the context of that organisational culture's formation (ibid.). Deference, conformity and obedience, while being stereotypical elements of military culture, were, for example, notably absent from NZDF personnel's understanding of professionalism. Moreover, the 'adventurer' or 'warrior' personality type, often identified as being central to professionalism in Anglo-Western armed forces, was similarly significantly moderated or absent in the narratives of NZDF personnel (Bondy 2005). Participants noted the need for such identities to be 'recalibrated' to allow for more constructive identities to be performed.

The value of effective communication, building trust and displaying patience, as well as being understanding and empathetic, are characteristics that challenge the warrior identity (Duncanson 2009) but are needed in complex situations such as this. Restraint, as an emerging indicator of professionalism amongst military personnel, has been suggested by Higate (2011: 330) to be linked not only to career experience and maturity but also to 'relational contrasting' between armed forces (where military personnel compare their practices with other military or security personnel). In these comparisons, aggressive behaviour was typically viewed as 'unprofessional' and deeply unhelpful (see Stevens and Greener, this volume). For the Kiwi personnel in the PRT, their role as a facilitator of development meant that professionalism was constructed around engagement and trust. 'Relational contrasting' was evident as many spoke about the differences they observed between their own approach and those of other militaries and civilian practitioners from other countries.

Professionalism was also evoked in discussions of accountability; accountability to both the people of Bamiyan and those of New Zealand. The desire to achieve 'real' development results was linked with the fact that the NZ PRT was a small unit, from a small country, with little guaranteed access to funding, meaning that those projects that they did undertake ought to be certain to provide value for the Afghan people and be sustainable. This sense of responsibility and connection was linked back to the importance of a foreseeable withdrawal of New Zealand troops; as one participant remarked, 'if you've got a small defence force, or civil defence organisation, or aid agency, wouldn't you be best to teach them [the local population] to do the job themselves?'

The presence of both the 'Anzac identity' and the 'professional identity' discourses in the reflections of personnel raises the question of how the two interact to influence what might be said to constitute a contemporary New Zealand military identity. NZDF personnel were potentially able to draw on these two distinct identity discourses in order to make sense of their experiences with development. However, it has also been argued that for individuals who occupy uncertain spaces 'the simultaneous existence of multiple systems that define our realities can cause cognitive dissonance' (Sultana 2014: 337). That is, personnel could potentially be unable to reconcile their two competing identities and might fail to comprehend how they could successfully engage in development practice.

Cognitive dissonance and identity

WHILE SCHOLARS HAVE CRITIQUED THE application of military force in attempts to bring about development, the personnel interviewed displayed an acute awareness of the difficulty inherent in defending this position. Their role as military actors in the development or humanitarian space was an extension of New Zealand's national and historical commitment to fairness, collective security and peaceful relations between states and peoples. In their narratives they would often return to examples of NZDF involvement in peacekeeping and reconstruction work in order to illustrate proficiency in such operations, in addition to reinforcing the differences between their own conduct and the conduct of other national militaries. Aspects of the Anzac identity were drawn upon to help emphasise ingenuity in developing solutions to material deficits in Afghan livelihoods, as well as to focus on egalitarian attitudes to practice.

This essentially allowed personnel to confirm the acceptability of their work as development actors. In instances where the acceptability of this work was challenged by civilian development practitioners, personnel indicated an ability to understand these contrasting perceptions, while also drawing on aspects of Anzac identity to reaffirm that the behavioural norms which underpinned their actions were fundamentally positive and constructive. Finally, in situations where personnel felt uncertain in their role as development practitioners, or where the structures of the PRT were insufficient in guiding their practice, exercise of agency was explained with respect to this identity, suggesting that responses in these instances were 'natural or normal' to NZDF personnel (this is further discussed later in this volume).

Discursive representations of the New Zealand-military identity as a professional identity were also available to personnel. The professionalism discourse presented, in most instances, a complementary identity for personnel to draw upon to achieve 'subjective composure'. Personnel were able to affirm their value as development practitioners as a result of their experiences in similar operating environments. Further, relational framing was employed to situate the New Zealand soldier as restrained and non-confrontational, an asset in the context of development where respectful conduct forms the foundation of productive partnerships. Finally, professional identity discourse involved an understanding of accountability in work, both to the New Zealand population as funders of the NZ PRT, and to the people of Bamiyan to ensure that development was ultimately sustainable.

The Anzac discourse is undoubtedly influential in shaping how NZDF personnel understand the collective characteristics that define their behaviour and differentiate them from others. In understanding themselves as professionals, however, personnel partially discard the 'everyman' civilian-soldier identity that is characteristic of the Anzac discourse. While the civilian-soldier, in the absence of formal training, has mythically proven him/herself capable of mastering a presented task, the professional soldier recognises the necessity of a degree of organisational support when required to undertake non-standard activities, such as development facilitation. In this respect the Anzac identity constitutes a useful resource for personnel to understand their approach to development work as both an individual and as part of the collective; however, the Anzac identity remains primarily personal and is predicated on its ability to exist and guide practice in the absence of organisational directives and structural support.

The professionalism discourse, in situations where military actors are held accountable for guaranteeing security and facilitating development, recognises that the application of the Kiwi way or a can-do attitude (as emphasised in the Anzac identity) is insufficient on its own. Personnel often remarked that they expected more structural guidance concerning their role as development practitioners. Further, the suggestion from several participants that the NZDF, in one way or another, relies on the reproduction of the Kiwi way in instances where organisational capacity is deficient or directives may still be in their formative stages, places the judgement and conduct of the individual at the fore of defining good development practice. In this respect professional identity also presents a discourse upon which personnel are able to draw to explain their approach to development work both as an individual and as part of the collective. However, unlike the Anzac identity, the professional identity expects organisational structures to be well formed and for learning to be clearly evident.

In understanding the New Zealand-military identity as a professional identity, personnel conveyed that they expected to be supported in the learning of new professional competencies such as development facilitation. This is underscored by the fact that development facilitation, project planning and structures for coordination between civilian agencies and military units were all areas that non-command-level personnel cited an interest in learning more about as a result of their experiences in Afghanistan. The link between professionalism and accountability caused personnel to feel frustrated when they were unable to ensure that development projects successfully translated into impact felt by communities. Ingenuity, while sufficient to bridge gaps in organisational structures within discursive representations of Anzac identity, was an unacceptable response within discussions of professionalism. One participant remarked that reliance on the ingenuity of individuals to ensure that development projects were successful cast New Zealanders as 'scavengers' rather than a well-trained, professional defence force. Another participant, too, reflected that he felt this was indicative of a problematic approach, suggesting that these deficiencies 'could have been ameliorated or mitigated with some good training, but I just don't think that training was available or considered at the time'.

From consideration of these two discursive identities available to NZDF personnel, it is evident that while the Anzac spirit is still pivotal in communicating the essence of a New Zealand approach, an understanding of military identity as a professional identity encourages personnel to question the degree of organisational support provided to aid in their capacity as facilitators of development. The contentious nature of civil–military integration exemplified by the PRT inhibits personnel from drawing on these discourses to fully achieve subjective composure. Instead, personnel used both identity discourses as resources to fill in the gaps of what it meant to them to be a New Zealander, a soldier, and a development practitioner.

Referring to notes written in preparation for the interview, one participant suggested that the understanding of identity that New Zealanders took to Bamiyan constituted a 'force multiplier . . . for an army of our size and capability'. Force multiplication refers to attributes that make a military more effective at a given task (Cobane 2005). The presence of a New Zealand-military identity is significant insofar as it is understood by personnel to exist, retold in narratives of experience and reproduced by them in their practice. In the case of development work, identity constitutes not solely a resource for personnel to draw upon to achieve subjective composure but also a resource in the area of operations, not to be taken for granted. I would argue that the way that the identity of the New Zealand soldier is understood, at the individual and organisational levels, does not automatically make them good at development work. But rather as one participant suggested at one point, this identity has the potential to make them *better*, the question then becoming one of how to capitalise on this to develop resilient and sustainable capacity at an organisational level. As a participant concluded:

> I would hope that, you know, the next time, maybe somewhere in the future, we get involved in something like Bamiyan, that we use those people, their knowledge and their experience and training to help shape our plan, and help shape how we engage with other actors in that space, because, as you know, it's a complex space.

Conclusion

THIS CHAPTER HAS ATTEMPTED TO examine what doing development work in Afghanistan has meant for NZDF personnel and for how they conceive of their individual and collective identity. In being given responsibility for facilitating development in Bamiyan, personnel imagined and created meaning for themselves and others, shaping their own identity and how they were perceived through interaction, connection, practice and dialogue. The experiences here also speak to the military sociology literature more generally by identifying an emphasis on professionalism

— a defining trait preferred by certain sociologists (notably Huntington) over citizen-soldier models.

One of the consequences of this research is that it suggests that an opportunity exists for the NZDF to leverage off these pre-existing behavioural norms to enhance effectiveness in the field. That is, combining the best of the Anzac with the desire of the professional for constant improvement may help further NZDF objectives. The positioning of the PRT as accountable to the population of Bamiyan for development work facilitated by them underpinned an almost universal desire for more organisational support, professional development, and knowledge where development work was concerned.

This desire to make a difference in their work confirms Anna Simons' assessment that, in her experience, 'most [military personnel] are fully vested in the conviction that things can be improved. Otherwise, not even the most cynical of them would be sticking it out when, in today's all-volunteer force, none of them has to' (2012: 236). This conviction invites a more concerted engagement within militaries with critical approaches to their practice, while promoting the establishment or augmentation of programmes concerning development theory, policy and practice.

Afghan officer cadets in Bamiyan practise tactical exercises without troops.

04

New Zealand Military as Peacekeepers: International perceptions

Peter Greener

> We have a reputation around the world for our professionalism, training and skills. We set ourselves high standards and we get things done. — Lt. Gen. Tim Keating, Chief of Defence Force (2014: 2)

OVER 20 YEARS AGO, MILITARY historian John Crawford noted that New Zealand military personnel 'who have participated in peace-support operations have established an excellent record, which rests on impartiality, high professional standards, and an outstanding ability to work with men and women from many other nations often in very difficult circumstances' (1996: 48). Almost a decade later these sentiments were echoed by the then Deputy Chief of Navy, Commodore David Anson. He declared that 'It is through this willingness, this attitude to doing more than is asked, and the quality of our people, trained and equipped to do a job and do it well, that New Zealand has earned our good reputation on the world stage' (2005: 27).

More recently Deputy Chief of Air Force, Air Commodore Darryn Webb, commenting on his time at the Centre for Defence and Strategic Studies in Canberra, noted, 'Our ability as a Defence Force . . . never ceased to amaze . . . [and] our cultural, professional and motivational value-adding ability was noteworthy to our partners' (2016: 3). Nevertheless, the evidence has thus far remained anecdotal, with little comprehensive research that could potentially confirm, or otherwise, these positive perceptions.

This chapter explores what it is that New Zealand's military and civilian partners on operations value about NZDF personnel, and what they feel it is that helps define our contribution. Based on interviews with a range of partner personnel, this chapter highlights a number of characteristics that were consistently identified as being associated with the NZDF. It therefore adds to the discussion of identity begun by Harding and others in this volume by asking how others view the New Zealand military, and concludes with observations that may help further enhance the work undertaken by NZDF personnel on deployment.

The research project

THE RESEARCH PRESENTED IN THIS chapter is based on 30 personal interviews undertaken on field visits to three New Zealand deployments overseas between 2012 and 2013. These interviews took place with members of the Multinational Force and Observers (MFO) in the Sinai (at North Camp, Sinai and Rome Headquarters); the International Stabilisation Force and the United Nations Integrated Mission in Timor-Leste (Dili); and the United Nations Truce Supervision Organisation in Israel, with interviews at UNTSO HQ in Jerusalem and Observer Group Golan (OGG) in Tiberias. Brief summaries of these missions follow to outline the context within which NZDF personnel have operated and are operating. Before we begin, however, it is important to reflect on how this research was carried out.

The opening chapters in this volume (Harding and Guesgen) pursue an anthropological approach. This requires deep ethnographic work, sometimes living with those communities that you are seeking to understand. Morris's work, however, introduced us to semi-structured interviews as a way of attempting to understand key themes underpinning how military personnel understand their roles as development actors. This chapter pursues a similar approach. Semi-structured interviews were used for data gathering, the material from which was recorded in field texts. Qualitative content analysis (Zhang and Wildemuth 2009) was then used to identify themes that would illustrate the qualities, good or not so good, that Kiwis displayed on operations.

In terms of how interviewees were chosen, purposive sampling was used to identify potential participants. Participants were chosen relevant to the particular operation, and provided with a letter of introduction from the assistant chief of personnel, NZDF. In the Middle East, senior commanders, civil and military, and military observers were approached by the respective New Zealand senior national officer (SNO) on the researcher's behalf, while the researcher wrote directly to the civilian leadership at the office of the director-general of the MFO in Rome. In Timor-Leste, interviews with Australian military personnel were facilitated by the New Zealand senior national officer; interviews with civilians who had current or previous experience with NGOs were facilitated by Dr Anna Powles; and Colonel Martin Dransfield, chief military liaison officer for UNMIT, organised meetings with senior military and civilian leaders.

There are some limitations in the research. Only three operational visits were conducted, and only one interviewee was a woman. Another limiting factor is that participants were approached by New Zealanders. This potentially creates some issues regarding the nature of the interview — that is, having the potential interviewees approached by an SNO, having the research supported directly by the NZDF and being an employee of the NZDF at the time creates a context within which certain views might be more or less likely to be expressed. In light of this, then, claims made here are to be treated as indicators of certain likely characteristics rather than as concrete 'facts' about NZDF personnel on operations. Moreover, in further attempts to ensure that ethical needs were met, it was made clear to all potential interviewees that participation was voluntary; having said this, there appeared to be a genuine keenness to participate. Lieutenant Colonel P, for example, a very experienced officer from the former Yugoslavia, asserted that 'I am 100 per cent soldier, I am an ex-Yugoslav soldier. When your CLOATA [Chief of Liaison Amman–Tel Aviv] said you wanted to see me, I wanted to meet with you.'

Thirty participants in total were interviewed, with interviews lasting anything from 30 minutes to an hour and a half. With the exception of one expatriate, all participants were non-New Zealanders. Almost all of the interviewees had good English language skills; two had the assistance of an interpreter. Just over a third of the participants were from the Americas, more than a third from Timor-Leste and Oceania, and the balance from Europe. As might be expected with the types of mission, the majority of the military officers were at lieutenant colonel or equivalent (E) rank, or major or equivalent (E) rank. All but two of the military personnel interviewed were army. The transcripts of those interviews inform this research; any quotations that lack an in-text credit are drawn from those transcripts.

In considering how to use, understand and present data gathered from such interviews, Zhang and Wildemuth (2009) suggest that when presenting the results of content analysis a balance between description and interpretation should be sought. Denzin (as cited in ibid.) noted that description provides background and context and should therefore be rich and thick. Beginning with brief overviews and summaries of the missions in question (UNTSO, MFO, UNMISET/INTERFET/UNTAET/ISF/UNMIT), the following sections therefore aim to achieve that balance between description and interpretation in examining the roles and identified characteristics of NZDF personnel on mission.

Brief overviews of the three missions

The United Nations Truce Supervision Organisation

SPEAKING TO THE UNITED NATIONS General Assembly at the time of the proposed partition of Palestine in 1947, Sir Carl Berendsen, then New Zealand's minister in Washington, stated that:

> if the United Nations assumes . . . responsibility for the partition of Palestine, it should unquestioningly assume, at the same time, the duty of protecting the population of the country against any disturbance that might result, and should prepare itself accordingly (NZ Government 1947: 144).

In the event, that level of protection never eventuated. While the General Assembly agreed to a resolution for the partition of Palestine, the plan proved to be unworkable. The British relinquished their mandate on 14 May 1948 and the state of Israel was declared. The following day fighting broke out, with Palestinians supported by Arab neighbours. The conflict continued until a truce was called for by the UN Security Council on 29 May. It was decided that the truce should be monitored by a group of unarmed military observers, the United Nations Truce Supervision Organisation (UNTSO), and the first observers were deployed in June 1948. The area of operations was to cover Israel, Lebanon, Syria, Jordan and Egypt.

In April 1954 New Zealand was elected chair of the UN Security Council, at a time when UNTSO was to be expanded. Just as with Bosnia some 40 years later, there was an expectation that New Zealand, as a strong supporter of the United Nations, would fulfil its obligations. New Zealand sent its first two Territorial Force United Nations Military Observers (UNMOs) to UNTSO in May 1954. By 1957 the New Zealand secretary of external affairs was to write to the acting minister of external affairs observing that 'New Zealanders are regarded as particularly good at this kind of work, which requires a high degree of initiative, coolness and tact in situations which, if mishandled, could lead to an outbreak of hostilities' (cited in M. Simons 2001).

Although in 2001 Squadron Leader Murray Simons was to say that 'the mission is not demanding and many see their tour as a year off from work' (ibid.: 14), this has most certainly not been the case since 2006, when conflict erupted between Hezbollah and the Israeli Defence Force, and Tyre came under heavy shelling and bombing.

UNTSO currently has two observer groups: Observer Group Lebanon (OGL) in south Lebanon and Observer Group Golan (OGG) operating on both the Israeli and the Syrian sides of the Golan Heights.

The number of New Zealand observers posted to UNTSO over the past 53 years has varied between four and 10 personnel at any one time, and over the time of the operation more than 360 unarmed New Zealand military observers have served in UNTSO (McArthur 2016). Three New Zealand Army officers have been Chief of Staff (commanding officer) of UNTSO. Colonel John Fisher served from 1993 to 1994; Major General Clive Lilley from 2004 to 2006; and Major General Dave Gawn (former Chief of Army) took up his post in September 2015. There are currently 384 personnel supporting the mission, 150 of them military observers supplied by 26 countries.

The Multinational Force and Observers

ON ANZAC DAY 1982, a small group of 36 New Zealanders, 29 from the Royal New Zealand Air Force and seven from the New Zealand Army, prepared to take up their duties in the Sinai in Egypt as part of the newly formed Multinational Force and Observers (MFO). The MFO is a peacekeeping 'coalition of the willing' brought together (before the term 'coalition' became common currency) by the willingness of the previously warring states of Egypt and Israel and the encouragement of the United States. As an Anzac contingent they were to provide a Rotary Wing Aviation Unit with eight Australian and two New Zealand UH-1H 'Huey' helicopters, which would operate in the desert for the following four years. Although responsibilities have changed over time, that modest contribution of Kiwi personnel has continued unbroken for 35 years, helping maintain peace in a region that had seen three wars between Egypt and Israel in the 15 years prior to 1982 and the establishment of the MFO (P. Greener 2012). The MFO is based in two camps; el Gorah in the north is 20 kilometres inland from the Mediterranean Sea and perilously close to the jihadist stronghold of el Arish, while the south camp is near Sharm el Sheikh, overlooking the Red Sea.

Never larger than a contingent of 50, New Zealanders have played a central role in one of the most volatile and unpredictable regions of the world. Currently there are 26 New Zealand personnel deployed as part of the MFO; they provide a transport section of 12 to operate and drive vehicles as required by the MFO and they provide a Training and Advisory Team (TAT) of eight personnel. Each year New Zealand drivers cover on average almost 357,000 kilometres and the TAT trains over 1800 personnel from all 12 nations that are involved with the MFO (Martin 2013). There are also a number of headquarters staff, in particular the deputy chief of operations, who has responsibility for coordinating the operational activities of the MFO. Since 1982 some 1378 New Zealanders have served with the MFO (McArthur 2016: 21), and New Zealand has provided two force commanders of the MFO: Lieutenant General Donald McIver, who served as force commander from March 1989 to March 1991, and Major General Warren Whiting, who served from March 2010 to March 2014.

At the time of its twentieth anniversary, the MFO was described by the *RSA Review* (October 2002) as 'that almost forgotten peacekeeping operation'; but the circumstances of its mission have changed significantly in recent years (P. Greener 2012). With increasing numbers of attacks on Egyptian forces across the Sinai and a growing insurgency by a faction of the Islamic State (including the downing of a Russian airliner with the death of 224 passengers in November 2015), the role of the MFO is now more important than ever. However, increasing attacks on MFO personnel led to the USA transferring many of its troops from el Gorah to

Sharm el Sheikh in April 2016, along with NZDF forces, and future border monitoring by remote sensors was being considered (Hennigan 2016).

Timor-Leste

WHEN THE PEOPLE OF EAST Timor voted overwhelmingly for independence in 1999, a tidal wave of violence spread across the country, perpetrated by Indonesian-backed militia. In September 1999, New Zealand hosted the Asia-Pacific Economic Cooperation (APEC) summit. Initially it had been thought that East Timor would be a side issue at the meeting, but by the time President Bill Clinton had arrived the stakes had increased. Clinton had warned that if the violence in East Timor did not end then Indonesia 'must invite — it must invite — the international community to assist in restoring security' (as cited in P. Greener 2009).

In terms of planning for deployment to East Timor, at first New Zealand had considered sending a company of troops, about 120, as part of an international force, but ultimately a battalion group was committed, working alongside the Australians in a highly demanding environment. Over the following 15 years 4855 Kiwis were to serve in East Timor (McArthur 2016: 21).

In late September 1999 the Kiwis arrived in Dili to work as part of the Australian-led International Force East Timor (INTERFET), and by October a detachment had moved to one of the most dangerous border areas, Suai in Cova Lima province. By the end of October 1999 the first of what was to be six battalion groups had arrived, and some 1100 Kiwi personnel were involved in operations. Troops on the ground were to be supported by both the navy and the air force, and a helicopter squadron and a frigate were deployed throughout. At this time the mission had transitioned to the United Nations Transitional Administration in East Timor (UNTAET). The years 1999–2001, as East Timor moved slowly towards independence, were to be testing for the Kiwis. Shortly after the second battalion group had arrived, Private Leonard Manning was shot dead by militia on 24 July 2000. Two Kiwis had already died on the mission, with a third non-combat fatality in 2001 (Crawford and Harper 2001). Yet by the time the New Zealanders were drawing down following independence in May 2002, the nascent country was much more stable. The New Zealand battalion left in November that year, leaving a small group of 25 personnel in country. By now the mission had become the United Nations Mission of Support in East Timor (UNMISET), and three years later, in May 2005, UNMISET closed. The last of the Australian peacekeepers left Timor-Leste the following month.

This drawdown of personnel was, however, to be short-lived; increasing tension between the Timorese military and the police led to rioting breaking out in Dili in May 2006. Xanana Gusmão, the president of Timor-Leste, asked the Australians for assistance, and on 25 May 2006 New Zealand indicated that the NZDF would deploy an initial 120 troops in support of the Australian-led International Stabilisation Force (ISF) and the new United Nations Integrated Mission in Timor-Leste (UNMIT). New Zealand troops were to stay in numbers until December 2012, when the ISF withdrew. Five NZDF personnel remain in Timor-Leste under the Mutual Assistance Programme, providing mentoring to the Falintil-Forcas Defensa Timor Lorosa´e (F-FDTL), the Timor-Leste defence force.

HAVING OUTLINED THE NATURE OF the missions under discussion for the purposes of this chapter, and having identified New Zealand's quantitative contributions to those missions, we can now consider the qualitative contribution — the value that NZDF personnel brought to bear. In this we begin with a narrative description of the roles played by those personnel before moving to consider broader patterns in the ways in which those personnel were viewed by others.

The experience of Kiwis on the ground

WE NOW REVIEW SOME OF the roles played by NZDF personnel in recent missions, and explore some of the views and opinions expressed by representatives of other nationalities working or serving alongside these personnel. This section, therefore, examines the experience of Kiwis, both from the point of view of some of the developments faced by Kiwi personnel in the field and through others' experiences of interacting with those Kiwi personnel. Looking to UNTSO, the MFO and Timor, this section therefore begins to draw attention to the characteristics valued both within the NZDF and by others working with them.

Major S. of OGG emphasised that:

> I've had twenty-two years in the army. I've had extensive experience with the Kiwis. Kiwis are such positive people — so enthusiastic, so friendly, even after being shelled and kidnapped. They have a real ground-level assessment of the situation, a human response but a superb reaction that shows integrity and reflects so well on their country. If I had to choose a nationality to work with after what I've experienced I'd always choose a Kiwi.

Major S. had been a colleague of two Kiwis while posted to UNTSO. One was a Royal New Zealand Navy officer with whom he had worked in Syria and who had been detained by an armed faction. The other was a New Zealand Army officer, psychologist Captain Alia Bojilova. When interviewed for an article in *Army News* Captain Bojilova noted that being a military psychologist had its challenges, but that 'you get to see what makes resilience in action' (Martin 2014: 2). Writing in an article in *Golan: The UNDOF Journal* on 'The Countless Sources of Stress in the Ever-changing Face of the UNTSO Golan Mission', Captain Bojilova described the impact of being 'kidnapped', 'taken hostage', 'shelter-bound', 'held at a gun point' and 'hijacked', and of experiencing 'direct and indirect fire', 'break-ins', 'threatening of UN personnel' and 'hostile behaviour' (Bojilova 2013: 18). What she didn't mention was that she herself was at the centre of these experiences on two occasions.

Early in 2013 Captain Bojilova, Major S. and one other observer from OGG came under artillery fire in their observation post while monitoring an engagement between Syrian government forces and anti-government militia. The observers were forced to take cover for 36 hours until a ceasefire could be agreed, and Captain Bojilova's calm response to the crisis led the senior officer to suggest that he 'would put my life under her command in any situation of stress'. Just a few weeks later, on 14 May, Captain Bojilova and two other observers were kidnapped and held for three hours before release. Major S. suggested that Captain Bojilova would have been an asset, and that potentially it could have been she 'who got them out safely, because she could connect with the rebels. In our situation she built confidence between the UNMOs and the rebels to achieve the goal.' On 14 July 2014 Captain Alexandrina Alexandrova Bojilova, Royal New Zealand Army Education Corps (RNZAEC), was awarded one of the Chief of Defence Force's inaugural Meritorious Service Medals.

Similarly trying situations arose for NZDF personnel serving in the MFO. New Zealander Major General Warren Whiting had originally taken command of the MFO in March 2010 for a two-year term; this was then twice extended, and Major General Whiting eventually handed over to his successor in March 2014. At his farewell the MFO director-general, Ambassador David Satterfield, highlighted that Major General Whiting had served the MFO 'for four years that have been by far the most challenging since our inception. He has every reason to be proud of his many contributions to our mission of peace . . .' (MFO 2014).

During Whiting's term in March 2012 the MFO's North Camp at el Gorah, 16 kilometres from the Israeli border and 37 kilometres south-east of El Arīsh, was blockaded by armed Bedouin for eight days. Some six months later the camp perimeter was breached by 60 gunmen, and eight peacekeepers were wounded before a stand-down was negotiated. With the support of the Egyptian Army, which had arrived with 50 tanks and armoured vehicles, the attackers were dispersed.

Conditions in the Sinai deteriorated further following the removal of President Mohamed Morsi in July 2013, and Egypt sought Israeli approval to increase its presence on the peninsula. For some, this meant that the liaison role provided by the MFO was more invaluable than ever.

Noting that 'this mission is seen as having an essential calming function', a senior officer at MFO HQ emphasised the value of Major General Whiting having had prior service with the MFO, suggesting that Whiting was 'extremely successful' given that the success of the liaison system 'depends on personalities. If we have a force commander who will set regular meetings, and use those to draw people out, then we have a real advantage, and Warren achieves that.' Another experienced official suggested that Whiting had managed to 'establish confidential relationships' beyond professional relationships and that '[h]e's been able to adjust to different cultural values; Israelis are Western in their outlook, Egyptians more traditional, and General Whiting can cross the cultural divide. He can deal with a culture which is not his.'

Similar comments about culture have been discussed in previous chapters in this volume, and they also arose in discussions about New Zealand's role in East Timor. Two Timorese civilians who had worked with NGOs were forthright in their recollection of New Zealand's contribution, the first commenting:

> As soon as the Kiwis were in an area they sought to understand local structures; they respected local chiefs, priests and teachers. At the time of their initial deployment, apart from their role in military stabilisation, they built relationships so you continually felt safe. They reinforced local leadership. The community felt that the Kiwis were 'older brothers'; they became embedded in

A Multinational Force and Observers (MFO) supply tanker.

> the local community, so it was hard to create violence when they had such a relationship. They brought warmth and calmness. You clearly saw the respect Pākehā or Māori Kiwis gave.
>
> The Kiwis were a modern force fiercely proud of their culture (maybe the Irish Rangers came close in terms of qualities), and the Kiwis are ferocious warriors. I remember when you lost Private Manning — the tohunga [spiritual leader] who gave prayers so his soul could go to heaven. That left a very strong bond between people. The Western Timorese really respected that. It's the spiritual qualities that mark the Kiwis out. As I said, a modern army, but they were warriors and they had a moral compass. The Kiwis demonstrated mateship — they really look after people. There's honour in that it's about knowing that you're there for a higher cause.

The second, now a successful businessman in Dili, was keen to share more observations:

> How would I describe the Kiwis? Not reasonably good, not quite good, but *very* good. Your guys were posted to Suai; to my point of view I felt, this is good, we'll be safe. The Aussies were in the west, and I felt the frontier was being protected by two very professional militaries. I was working at the time with internally displaced persons (IDPs). I waited for the green light from the Kiwis before helping people return to their home areas. I met soldiers across all ranks, warrant officers, sergeants, majors, they were just all so professional. The Kiwi military weren't just military, they were humanitarians. They provided both security and humanitarian support at the same time. They were very friendly, yet gave a clear message, 'You mess with us, and we'll mess with you.' The Timorese welcomed that.

Over 13 years later, as the Kiwis were preparing to leave in December 2012, senior members of the F-FDTL, the Timor-Leste defence force, echoed a number of the above sentiments. One senior officer noted:

> My officers feel more confident working with Kiwis. It's to do with culture; New Zealanders are more flexible than others. The interaction with us is very good, though hard to explain. Perhaps it's because Kiwis are more patient, more open, more humble. When you're referring to those of European heritage, New Zealanders are different.

Another senior commander emphasised the perceived generosity of NZDF personnel, suggesting that Kiwis express that generosity

> . . . by truly understanding the other side, and that's a special attitude. I can see that in all of the Kiwis; they have a proper sensibility; they approach us in a soft way. That's a real strength when the people need gestures of solidarity. It's a way of encouraging others to have hope, to feel safe.

He also asserted that Kiwi personnel demonstrated 'integrity, a sense of humility. They're respectful; for example they know exactly how to behave, how to act', but he also noted that '[t]hey want to interact but they cannot talk'. That is, Kiwi personnel did not necessarily have any local language capability.

That important point aside, the former president of Timor-Leste, José Ramos-Horta, made note of one development that underscored how NZDF personnel were viewed within the country. He said:

> In 2006 when I wanted Alfredo [Reinado, rebel leader] to surrender, he said he would only surrender to Kiwi troops — he

> trusted them. Even the rebel soldier trusted them. New Zealand is perceived as not taking sides, being neutral, being fair. Over all of these years I've never had a single complaint from the people, the police or the army about Kiwi troops.

Making sense of these perceptions

THE ABOVE SECTION RELAYED SOME select commentaries about the characteristics of NZDF personnel. This section now looks to identify sub-themes (codes), patterns and overarching themes (categories) — a social science research approach commonly used in political science — using the raw data from all 30 participants.

The questions that informed the semi-structured interviews were intended to:

- identify the qualities that Kiwis brought to a mission
- understand why those qualities were valuable
- discover what areas of development New Zealand military peacekeepers needed to attend to.

In considering how to understand the raw data gathered from interviews, Ryan and Bernard (2003: 100) note that, 'In writing field notes the researcher acts as a kind of theme filter, choosing (often subconsciously) what data are important to record and what data are not. In this sense, producing field notes is a process of identifying themes.' From producing field notes, the next approach used here is a mix of summative content analysis (which means starting with the counting of unique words) and conventional qualitative analysis (where categories or themes were drawn inductively from the material). Some researchers, such as Miles and Huberman (as cited in Ritchie 2001), suggest that qualitative analysis could involve a number of phenomena including data reduction (simplification and abstraction of data) and conclusion drawing —

New Zealand soldiers on patrol in Timor-Leste.

gradually forming meaning from that data. In this particular case, then, the reduced data was analysed and then structured around the themes that emerged.

As discussed by Ryan and Bernard (2003), however, identifying themes does not provide a unique or total solution. Dey (cited in ibid.) has highlighted that 'there is no single set of categories [themes] waiting to be discovered. There are as many ways of "seeing" the data as one can invent' (103). The following themes (categories) and sub-themes (codes), with supporting text, are therefore those identified by the researcher as having significance due to their repetitive nature and the emphasis placed on these by the participants themselves. These themes include: professional attributes, personal qualities, cultural appreciation, attitudes, and areas for further development.

Professional attributes

INTERVIEWEES VOLUNTEERED A NUMBER OF descriptors for their experience of their Kiwi colleagues. Certain terms were repeatedly used, such as 'professional', 'get things done', 'mission focused', 'competent' and 'good operators' — terms that related to an overarching theme (or category) of 'professional attributes'. Indeed, the professional qualities of Kiwis were often specifically referred to, as the Dutch officer from UNTSO highlighted:

> In difficult situations, I don't see panic, I see professionalism: 'No panic, no worries.' Both of the Kiwis I worked with have their feet on the ground. They think things over and make a good analysis. Back in July–August last year they were at an OP with a Syrian Liaison Officer, a Norwegian woman and a Slovenian guy. There were four people in a car, which was stopped by rebels. I heard screaming, but due to the professionalism of the Kiwi officer they really de-escalated the situation.

Linked with this professionalism, something already noted in Morris's chapter (this volume), was the perception of the Kiwis as 'good operators'. This ability to join a mission and readily contribute was seen as Kiwis adding value. An experienced Swedish officer noted:

> This is my fourth mission; I was in Bosnia in '96, Iraq in 2005, and UNTSO OGL in 2009; I was with the MFO for four months also. I have contact with the line UNMOS and have a lot to do with the Kiwis. (Alia is deputy team leader.) The quality of their operational capability is very high and they come well prepared. They only have to adapt to the particularities of this mission, and they are very quick to adapt. Their dedication to professional work is very high and their dedication to co-operation with their other colleagues is very high . . . I've never seen that they've lacked any kind of training or knowledge at all.

When it came to adding value, further appreciation of the New Zealanders was identified by the sub-theme of 'get things done' (echoing Harding, this volume). This was once more apparent across each of the missions, captured by the comments of officers serving with the MFO. A Norwegian officer noted, 'The difference is the Kiwis say, "Yes, we can do." They have a "Can do, will do" attitude . . . and take the initiative' (again a theme spoken to in the chapter by Fish et al., this volume), while a Canadian MFO officer commented:

> They're great self-starters — hire and forget. They take ownership of their jobs and are very proactive. We like to see that — it's nice to know you can give a task and it'll get done, and you know it'll be done right.

The sub-themes of professionalism and getting things done, and done right, highlighted the importance of Kiwis being 'competent'. Also with the MFO, an officer from Colombia highlighted that '[y]our planning and ops guys are really smart — you realise that they have great knowledge. They have credibility.' An American officer in the same mission added, 'They know what the job is about, they bring good skill sets. I really can't identify any deficits,' while an Australian officer in Timor-Leste agreed, saying, 'Invariably Kiwis are highly competent and know their job.'

The final two sub-themes of 'mission focused' and 'warriors' (see Derbyshire, this volume, on the latter) were emphasised in the MFO and in Timor-Leste, and the sentiments of those who identified these attributes were summed up by another Canadian officer with the MFO:

> Your guys are . . . mission focused, Kiwi focused and professional in everything they do. These are committed professional warriors (even with the odd sailor and airman!). It gives confidence to others.

As the conversations with participants progressed, it became clear that there were more layers to what it was they appreciated about their Kiwi colleagues. The next theme then identified a number of particular 'personal qualities'.

Personal qualities

NEW ZEALAND MILITARY PERSONNEL WERE seen as having a range of important personal qualities: they were viewed as honest, with integrity; had an openness in their relationships and were dedicated in their work; and were respectful and acted with humility.

Openness and integrity were both highlighted by the Swedish UNMO at OGG-Tiberias:

> They are very open and don't keep their distance. They are what they are and they have nothing to hide. I can be sure that what

> they say is the truth; they have very high integrity and that's very satisfying for me. Some UNMOs just work to get the positions they want and expect; they seek to gain influence because that's what their country tells them to do. Sometimes I have to ask — 'Is this you? Are you dedicated to this work, or is someone else asking you?' With the Kiwis there's none of that. What you see is what you get.

Perhaps one quality identified that surprised more than most was that of humility. Identified in each of the missions, a senior Danish civilian working in Timor-Leste echoed the comments noted previously by Timorese senior officers and spoke to its importance: '(Your) people come with a sense of humility . . . I've seen that with the Kiwis and it goes down well here.' Respect also came through strongly, and very often that was linked with another identified theme, that of cultural appreciation.

Cultural appreciation

THIS THEME WAS APPARENT BASED on a simple word count, though inductive analysis of text highlighted just how prevalent this theme was. While appreciation of culture was clearly identified as a quality of the Kiwis, the emphasis on this aspect was so strong that it warranted a separate theme. From the very first set of interviews, the importance of the Kiwi awareness of cultural appreciation came through clearly. An American civilian with the MFO highlighted this:

> When it comes to qualities, there's a clear appreciation of diversity of culture. The Kiwis bring that strongly and that extends into a multinational operation such as this. Being able to work across cultures is key in this environment.

These sentiments were echoed by his Canadian colleague, who said,

'Your value structure is different from the Australians'. Your inculcation of native culture into army culture is unique. Māori culture is there and you can access it as a mission culture.' The importance of mission success being enhanced by the ability to appreciate other cultures was noted by the Kiwi expatriate in Timor-Leste: 'Flexibility is a major characteristic, which stems from cultural understanding and an ability to adapt to context, demand, and a range of different groups. The Kiwis were able to work with local power structures' — this adaptation providing hope to the notion that gender equality (Derbyshire, and Stevens and Greener, this volume) is achievable.

It is perhaps important to note here, though, as highlighted by Tabor (2016), that there is a difference between cross-cultural appreciation and cross-cultural competence. This will be discussed further under the theme of 'areas for further development'. Before coming to that, though, there is one further theme linked to 'qualities'.

Attitudes

IN IDENTIFYING WHAT ELSE HELPED New Zealand military personnel to work with others, and rounding out the factors that contributed to the value of Kiwis to a mission, a range of important attitudes was also identified — including informality, an easy-going nature, and a relationship-building emphasis. These attitudes were invoked by a Finnish officer with UNTSO, who declared:

> I've been here eleven months and have worked both with and under Kiwis. You're not strict, you're more flexible. The informality makes you easier to connect with and that's really helpful, yet when you need to be formal you can be. In general everyone likes the Kiwis — even the Canadians are more formal. I can't find anything negative to say. Whoever is selecting your guys is doing a great job.

Similar observations were made by officers with the MFO. The Norwegian officer noted:

> I find New Zealanders very easy to work with as we are very similar with little bureaucracy. The Kiwis are informal, not tied by regulations. We can both take the initiative on the ground without seeking higher guidance. In contrast the Australians are characterised by formality, they're much more formal and follow the regulations.

This sentiment was echoed by one of his American colleagues: 'Kiwis are relaxed, they don't get tense. They are so much more at ease than the Aussies. Kiwis are well suited because they bring a good attitude.' In Timor-Leste the Danish civilian added, 'I've seen with many Kiwis their ability to reach out, to gain the trust of the people.'

Positive attitudes and commendable qualities were identified by all of the participants, but, as noted earlier, one of the elements the research sought to discover was the areas of development New Zealand military peacekeepers needed to attend to.

Areas for further development

THE FIFTH THEME IDENTIFIED IN this research was then (unsurprisingly) 'areas for further development', though the areas that needed development were perhaps something of a surprise. While a number of interviewees indicated that they couldn't identify any areas for improvement, some were keen to assist.

In identifying areas for further development, at times there was a clear differential between officers and soldiers. This was not necessarily the case when it came to language. In the MFO a South American officer had interesting observations. 'Your young drivers are as good as my more experienced guys,' he said. 'But I do wish they could speak properly.' His

Norwegian counterpart clarified what this meant when I spoke with him. 'Language is an issue — sometimes the Kiwis speak too quickly, and that coupled with Kiwi words makes it a challenge.'

This was, interestingly, mirrored by comments from a senior officer in Timor-Leste. 'The senior officers communicate well with everyone but, if you're going to the Middle East, you really should speak more slowly. Here it's "Kia Ora Kiwi!"' In looking at speaking a host nation language, a Timorese civilian noted, 'The only issue is language. Please, pick interpreters who can speak proper English, then have someone who can check them out. Too often the interpreters would give the wrong message.' He then added, 'If only, if only some of your guys had spoken Tetum . . .' As if to underscore the point, another senior officer said, 'As for improvements, well, if more could speak Tetum . . .'

In looking at behaviour, perhaps it is no surprise that it was the behaviour of the ordinary soldiers, rather than experienced officers, to which attention was drawn. Once again the Norwegian officer with the MFO commented:

> The senior officers are fully attuned, educated, and have an awareness of what you can and can't do. But the younger they get, the more difficult they can be. Young NCOs and soldiers have access to large amounts of alcohol and abuse it. It's not just a Kiwi thing.

However, it *is also* 'a Kiwi thing' and concerns about young Kiwis didn't just relate to alcohol. In contrast to his South American colleague, the other South American officer noted:

> [Your officers] have credibility, and the cultural element helps; where I have a little divergence is with the drivers — specifically their attitude. They are too fast in their thinking and they can

> look a little hostile. The drivers need better integration into the Force — they're too young. Maybe choose more mature soldiers with better cultural awareness. For the other Kiwis the cultural background is good.

Across the world in Timor-Leste, a Timorese civilian highlighted the crucial importance of young soldiers being aware of their responsibilities:

> After all of my good comments, what needs to be addressed?
>
> - Alcohol. You're a young soldier, you have a rifle, you have a beer in your hand — it's NOT OK. These are critical issues.
> - Fraternisation. As an 18-year-old away from home a beautiful girl is a temptation. BUT you are the big brother, you're not there to fall in love.
> - Don't fight amongst yourselves — it's not acceptable.

When it came to identifying areas for further development for officers, other than language there was only one readily identifiable area. In the MFO one senior commander had noted that the Kiwis he had worked with were confident and not afraid to voice their opinions. In contrast a senior officer with UNTSO, having noted how strongly humility came through as a personal quality, added a qualifying note:

> To a certain extent you need to be humble in this environment. When you come here you need to understand where you are, that you need a humble attitude to adopt new ideas. If you fail in that, you fail in everything. But in being humble, you shouldn't be too humble; perhaps there are times when you need to force your way through. Sometimes your guys need to be a little more assertive.

Once again, this sentiment was mirrored in Timor-Leste:

> When I look at successive Kiwi deputy commanders — the Aussies are always more prominent — I thought the Kiwis could be more assertive. Each week I felt, 'It would be nice to hear from the junior partner.'

Conclusion

THE INTENTION OF THIS RESEARCH was to explore what it is that our partners on operations, military and civilian, value about NZDF personnel and what they feel it is that helps define our distinctive contribution. There were limitations to the research because of the limited nature of the sample in this study. Nevertheless, participants brought a wide degree of experience of working with New Zealanders and were themselves representatives from across five continents, and there was a remarkable amount of consistency in the observations made, despite the differences inherent in each mission.

Kiwis are viewed by others as having a natural advantage by dint of their bicultural background, although emphasis was given to cultural appreciation and there is clearly room for improvement in cultural competence. The majority of NZDF personnel of all ranks are seen as committed, professional and respected warriors. However, young servicemen and -women need to be especially vigilant about their social behaviour. A tendency to speak too quickly and use Kiwi slang is not helpful, and Kiwi humour can be misunderstood as disrespectful. This is not something to which attention would ordinarily be drawn in pre-deployment training, but there would be benefit in doing so. These observations, though, contrast with the overwhelming impression that NZDF personnel seek to be humble, don't pretend to know what they don't, and seek local advice to fill in the gaps.

In Timor-Leste two particular issues emerged. The strongest request was that at least some unit personnel spoke the local language Tetum; the other was that young troops remember that they are viewed as 'guardians' and their behaviour should always reflect that responsibility. The 2014 Defence Assessment noted that '[i]t is likely that over the next ten years, New Zealand will deploy military and other assets in support of a Pacific Islands Forum member in crisis beyond standard disaster response support' (Ministry of Defence 2014a). Given this anticipation, it would be sensible for the NZDF to identify those personnel who have competence in the languages of the South West Pacific. Finally, the issue of humility versus assertiveness warrants further deliberation. Does one preclude the other or can both elements be developed? Do Kiwi leaders need more development here?

Overall it appears as if positive, Kiwi-held perceptions are in fact to a large part shared by those alongside whom NZDF personnel work. Kiwis are viewed as good operators, who are professional and mission-focused. They are seen as relaxed and easy-going, yet have a 'can do' attitude and are keen to get results. While eager to help support local communities and build relationships to help prevent violence, they are willing to fight as professional warriors when necessary in order to protect. Nonetheless, there remain clearly identified areas for improvement, which, if attended to, will prepare NZDF personnel to be even more competent peacekeepers in future operations.

05

The Kiwi PRT Experience in Afghanistan

M. K. Lauren

MOVING ON FROM OTHERS' PERCEPTIONS of Kiwi personnel at work, this chapter[1] seeks to relay the overall atmosphere and activities of a working military operation in contemporary and complex times. It tries to convey some of the experiences of military personnel in the field and to note some of the issues that carry on around these personnel. The focus is on the New Zealand Provincial Reconstruction Team (NZ PRT) in Bamiyan province, Afghanistan.

The province, of which Bamiyan town is the capital, sits in the central highlands in the middle of Afghanistan, and is comparatively isolated. The terrain around the town is dry, rugged and mountainous. For a Kiwi, Bamiyan has an alien feel to it, as if you had suddenly found yourself on the surface of the moon. Fine dust gets into everything — it ruined the gears in my camera lens while climbing the imposing 'PT Hill' that jutted up behind Kiwi Base (no mean feat to climb, at 2500 m above sea level).

The town of Bamiyan looks small from the top of the hill, although its population is 60,000. Housing consists of walled-off square courtyards with the accommodation incorporated into the walls. Easily visible north of the town was a wall of sheer cliffs stretching out to the west in which the giant niches where the Bamiyan Buddhas — infamously destroyed by

---

1. This chapter is solely the work of the author. Any views expressed in it are those of the author and do not necessarily represent official policy of the New Zealand Defence Force.

the Taliban in 2001 — stand empty. It is relatively easy to tunnel into these cliffs, and caves in them have been used as housing through the centuries, with external structures often incorporated. The base itself consisted of a collection of hut-like structures occupying a roughly rectangular area, surrounded by a wall of HESCO barriers — wire mesh containers covered in heavy-duty fabric and filled with whatever was available, mostly dirt and rocks.

It was within this unfamiliar and alien environment that Kiwi personnel were attempting to help provide security, support governance and facilitate development. This chapter has been drawn from a Defence Technology Agency work package commissioned by the then Commander Joint Forces (COMJ), Major General Dave Gawn. My visit to one rotation of NZDF personnel at the PRT in Afghanistan had an intentionally broad brief, and in part was conducted with the aim of trying to identify what the social sciences might have to offer to the understanding of operational performance (as per the trend in militaries internationally to look more carefully at the role of populations on operations — effectively seeing the population as 'the centre of gravity' in military terminology). Given that there is little public knowledge about the nature of New Zealand's commitment to Afghanistan, and given that this has been one of the NZDF's longest deployments, this chapter seeks to relay some of the major features of the deployment to Bamiyan to contribute to future debate.

Undertaking this research

INFORMATION FROM THIS VISIT WAS collected via interviews with PRT members, which were conducted informally for the purpose of reporting back to COMJ, rather than following the more demanding procedures that would be typically used for an academic social science study. However, to maintain the anthropological practice of protecting research participants (ASA 1999), personnel are not identified in this report. Generally, the interviewees were senior personnel or experts in their areas. Notes were also made of informal comments and observations outside of these interviews. These discussions shaped the information collected, both providing a context in which to interpret and test information via interviews with other personnel, and offering cues as to what kinds of question might be most interesting to ask and who might be most useful to talk to. From further informal discussions with other personnel back in New Zealand, it was found that many of the themes discovered during this particular rotation had commonalities with the experiences of other rotations in Afghanistan. Nonetheless, it needs to be recognised that the operations evolved over time as circumstances changed, and that this chapter focuses on a particular moment in time (see Hall 2010 for another account of life in the PRT).

This chapter first introduces the overall structure and main objectives of the NZ PRT. It then discusses the environment of the base and the area of operations, as well as noting the central importance of the 'human element' (as explored further in Wineera's chapter in this volume). The chapter then asks what personnel actually did, noting that the key task was security provision but that personnel could also get pulled into development roles, while also noting perceptions of Kiwi personnel. Finally, the chapter notes the difficulties in balancing a desire to achieve meaningful and lasting change while also fulfilling military roles, and the desire of personnel to improve their ability to do so.

Structure, location and objectives of the NZ PRT

AS RELAYED IN MORRIS'S CHAPTER in this volume, the term Provincial Reconstruction Team refers to a joint civilian–military unit, and there were several throughout Afghanistan. Each PRT was 'fitted' to the local situation, so the nature of the operations in Bamiyan reflected the peculiarities of that environment. The NZ PRT was an integrated civil–military team under one command. It could field up to five patrols, and used forward patrol bases to extend their reach and endurance. US PRTs tended to be smaller civil affairs teams supported by local combat units. UK PRTs operated in small patrols, but there was a clear organisational separation between the military and civilian components. The NZ PRT's mission was to strengthen the influence of the government in Bamiyan province by assisting with reconstruction, facilitating aid and providing security (Duxfield 2012). Hoadley (2015) provides a detailed description of the history, rationale and structure of the PRT.

The US handed the military lead for the Bamiyan PRT to New Zealand in 2003. The NZDF deployment was named Task Group CRIB and, though responsible to the NZDF COMJ and Chief of Defence Force, it formed part of the United States' Regional Command East Afghanistan.

The main base (Kiwi Base) was located in the Bamiyan district near the town of the same name. It housed NZDF, Ministry of Foreign Affairs and Trade (MFAT) officials, NZ Police, US personnel (military and USAID civilians), and a European Union police contingent (EUPOL). A Malaysian Army contingent also operated a medical facility in the town.

The province consists of six districts. Yakawlang district sits to the west, and Panjab and Warras to the south. To the north are the Sayghan and Kahmard districts. It was this latter district where the NZ PRT suffered its combat casualties. Forward operating bases (FOBs) existed in both Yakawlang (FOB Chunuk Bair) and Kahmard (FOB Romero).

The New Zealand operation shifted from a military to a civilian lead in 2010. An initial 'transition' process took place in July 2011. This involved the handing of responsibility for security for most of the province over to the Afghan National Police (ANP). NZDF was to focus its security efforts on the northern provinces, for which (partly due to ethnic tensions between different parts of the province) the ANP were arguably not yet ready. Under this civilian leadership, the NZ PRT interacted with the local provincial government using political rather than military norms. The

Bamiyan provincial government had the lead and set priorities for the province, with the role of the PRT being to offer guidance and negotiate matters relating to the use of New Zealand and foreign aid, as well as manage security issues that the ANP had not yet taken over.

According to the draft Bamiyan PRT Evolution Plan developed by the civilian director, the plan for the PRT was to focus on developing the local government's ability to deliver basic services to the province, while at the same time nurturing the ANP's ability to provide security. It recognised that, post-2013, the province would require ongoing international development assistance. Part of this strategy was to ensure that the local government not only took responsibility but was also given credit for achievements. It was hoped that this would encourage the local population to see their government, rather than the PRT, as the source of their basic needs.

Given these objectives, and building on Morris's previous chapter, it can usefully be asked what army personnel were tasked with doing in attempts to achieve these objectives, though we first consider what their working conditions at Kiwi Base and within the area of operations were like.

Kiwi Base and the operating environment

THE PERSONNEL IN KIWI BASE were well looked after, with good food choices — though the forward operating bases were more spartan. Personnel generally shared huts and, despite the small amount of personal space, these looked quite comfortable, with air-conditioning and heating units. Although there were communal lounges, most personnel seemed to spend their nights watching *South Park* and *Family Guy* in their huts on whatever devices were available. In some ways, to an outsider, it felt like a school camp. The Kiwis were also occasionally invited into the building housing the EU Police contingent. The interior of this building had the comforts of a modern office block, housing their accommodation and an open-plan office with a giant TV — perfect for watching live sport, thanks to the British broadcasting service operating in Afghanistan (the Kiwi accommodation also had this service).

The area of operations for the NZ PRT was approximately 100 by 150 kilometres. Although distances were seemingly short, the poor condition of the roads and the mountainous terrain meant that it could take a day to cross the province. Adding to this, the mean high and low temperatures fluctuate between about −10°C in the winter (but can get much colder) to around 26°C in the summer. This made movement in the winter particularly difficult, and added another level of complexity to a situation where the main security risk for the PRT typically lay in the northern districts of the province, where insurgent and criminal groups operated with the most freedom, and where strong relations between peacekeeping forces and the local population were paramount to efforts to diminish risk and increase security.

The NZ PRT arguably had a close relationship with the Bamiyan people and the province was one of the safest in Afghanistan. The province contained two major ethnic groups, Hazara (who are the majority within the province) and Tajik, although other groups were present (see Naval Postgraduate School source). Within the major groups there were subtle differences between subgroups, reflecting the at times daunting ethnic diversity of the province. The Hazara resided principally in the south and west, while the Tajiks represented the bulk of the population in the northern parts.

The Hazara have historically been oppressed within Afghanistan by other ethnic groups, because of religious differences owing to the fact that this group are predominantly Shia Muslims. The Hazara generally aligned with the Northern Alliance against the Taliban. When the Hazarajat (the area dominated by the Hazara people) was captured by the Taliban in 1998, the Hazara people suffered severe oppression and a number of massacres occurred, particularly in the Yakawlang district in 2001 (Amnesty International 2001). Moreover, in wider Afghanistan, the Hazara people had also become targets for the predominantly Pashtun Taliban (Rashid 2000; Goodson 2001).

A significant ethnic divide between the north and the south of the province was therefore potentially problematic for both the NZ PRT and the provincial government. One problem was that the security force within the province, the ANP, largely comprised ethnic Hazara and was hence less comfortable operating in the Tajik region. The local National Directorate of Security (NDS), on the other hand, was largely composed of personnel of Tajik origins, and therefore a more logical force to operate in the northern districts. It was a unit of the NDS that patrols from the NZ PRT went to assist in 2012, leading to the Battle of Baghak in which Lance Corporals Pralli Durrer and Rory Malone were killed and several other NZDF personnel injured (NZDF 2013).

The PRT director expressed the view that the areas of the province dominated by the Hazara posed little security risk, principally because of the atrocities experienced by this group at the hands of the Taliban. He noted that the strength of the relationship with the Hazara was such that if outsiders were spotted in the bazaar, then the PRT would be called. However, according to discussions with EUPOL personnel and other foreigners at the base, this also meant that the local people saw the NZ PRT as being there to look after the Hazara. A significant part of the deployment, then, was understanding the dynamics and desires of the local population.

Understanding the human element

A COMMON THEME OF DISCUSSIONS with military personnel was the need to build understanding of the local culture and environment before coming into the theatre. Many personnel said that preparation for deployment was largely self-driven, and that knowledge of the cultural terrain and cultural awareness was often not well developed amongst PRT members. Consequently, it could take several months to get their head around the environment. One NZDF member commented that occasionally there was even a lack of understanding that there were two principal ethnic groups in Bamiyan.

Remote regions in many parts of Bamiyan were still tribal societies. These were highly conservative and patriarchal, and there were ethnic influences on hierarchy. Furthermore, the nature of the society (and broken-down infrastructure and governance) meant that personal relationships were far more important than institutions. In the minds of locals, dealings were never 'just business'.

The difficulty many personnel had, particularly when first in theatre, lay in understanding that the various ethnic groups were all slightly different. Some ethnic information was available in theatre from cultural advisors and translators, and local employees could also be used as cultural advisors. There were concerns, however, that such people, being locals, might bring their own biases.

Identified by NZDF personnel as of the greatest need, therefore, were the following: a better awareness and understanding of the attitudes and demeanour of particular villages in the province; knowledge of what was normal, and an ability to recognise when things were not normal; better awareness of the social networks that existed within the province, how these worked and who the key influencers were; and better understanding of how the locals solved disputes and what the sources of tensions were. For example, young platoon leaders on patrol could be thrown into key leadership engagement without much training in cultural norms, dispute resolution or negotiation, albeit this might be mitigated by the influence of senior NCOs.

Nonetheless, overall NZDF personnel seemed highly aware of the 'hearts and minds' aspects of the operation, and it was evident that they saw it as important to understand the psychology of the local people (see Wineera, this volume). Various PRT members expressed the view that Afghan solutions were needed for Afghan problems. Foreign PRT members also noted the importance of understanding the human terrain, given that the social dynamics in the region were complex. The USAID chief described it as a question of knowing where a person came from and what that person's history was. Often not a lot of care and attention was put into that, and discontinuity between rotations added to this problem.

However, one of the US civilian staff with extensive experience in development work and Afghanistan felt that it was counter-productive for the military PRT members to try to get too far into the heads of the Afghans. The majority of the people in the region did not want to get involved in fighting and no amount of study would change this. It was important to keep in mind what the purpose of the PRT was: to provide security and to rebuild the province's infrastructure and the capabilities of the local government. Furthermore, in his observation he noted that some of the people involved in supplying cultural information did not necessarily have the right skills. Most staff noted that what was of importance was an ability to build relationships.

Finally, the six-month deployment period was seen by many as being too short for personnel to become fully effective. It was claimed that fresh staff were only just getting up to speed by the end of their tour. The environment was constantly evolving, so that even staff who had previously been deployed could struggle to get up to speed. It was also claimed that preparation in New Zealand prior to deployment was not having much of a mitigating effect on this situation.

Despite all of these issues, however, findings from this case study seem to also uphold the general assumption in New Zealand that the NZDF was doing creditable work. But just what was that work?

What did New Zealand Army personnel do?

NEW ZEALAND ARMY PERSONNEL ONLY partially contributed to training the ANP, as there was also a New Zealand and European police presence at Kiwi Base to train the local police to become the main security force (see Fish et al., this volume, as to why this was important). Predominantly, the New Zealand Army performed the traditional roles of deterrence and providing security for others via patrolling, intelligence gathering and, when necessary, kinetic operations. However, as noted by Morris (this volume), they were also drawn into the realm of development where some projects were either directly taken on or facilitated by various CRIB rotations.

The majority of the population of Afghanistan lives below the poverty line, and Bamiyan's relative isolation made economic development there more difficult. Development was seen by all of the PRT staff as an important tool in both supporting transition and disrupting insurgent activity — i.e. providing an incentive for the population to support the local government rather than the insurgency. Indeed, development was a key component of the PRT's plan, as reflected in comments from MFAT and USAID staff members. According to the USAID personnel, being an expert in development programmes required significant technical expertise. Enhancing the local government's capabilities was central to this. Thus organisations such as MFAT, NZAID and USAID aimed to provide technical assistance to the local government rather than just being mechanisms to provide funding.

Development priorities were managed via a provincial development board, with the PRT civilian leadership dealing with the governor on a daily basis. The most significant economic development work had been concentrated in the south. However, there were also concerns about the ability of the local government to maintain infrastructure, given the capability gaps and lack of administrative knowledge, lack of locally generated funding, and endemic corruption and incompetence. MFAT personnel recognised that development needed to go through the central government line ministries. Indeed, central government had a strong influence within the province, which could be problematic; for example, in managing problems such as local corruption.

The PRT also tracked where NGOs went so it could help to provide security where appropriate, although the information flow from some of these organisations was poor due to the suspicion some had of the military. The upshot of this was that there was poor coordination at times between the NGOs and the PRT. It also raised the question of ethics in relation to humanitarian assistance, as discussed briefly in Morris and Fish et al. (this volume).

Development was a source of contention between the military and civilian members of the PRT. Similarly to the sentiment described in Morris's chapter, the view was consistently expressed that the military did not have the time or the expertise to do development 'properly'. This was particularly so given that NZDF rotations were six-monthly, meaning that commanders needed to do something quickly if they were to have an impact during their tenure. Indeed, both New Zealand and US civilian members of the PRT were able to offer examples of where the relationship between the military and the civilian experts had gone wrong.

Moreover, some of the civilian PRT members expressed the view that development work integrated as part of a counterinsurgency (COIN) strategy did not work, and building something for somebody to 'buy security' was seen as a poor form of development. Rather, they felt that development should be a process of capability building. Building hospitals for which there were no doctors, or roads that no one maintained, could be counter-productive. For example, in considering where to build new roads it was important to look at population distributions, and how new roads might affect local commerce. A new road has the ability to attract new business to one bazaar at the expense of another. The USAID chief and others therefore suggested that the key was to encourage the locals to take the lead as often as possible in deciding priorities.

NZDF personnel also expressed concern over the ability to synchronise 'effects' (in essence, part of the influence tactics used by the military elements) with the actions of civilian personnel and NGOs. This was at least partly motivated by the desire to coordinate projects so as not to duplicate efforts. This included identifying what the issues were in each area and coming up with plans for how to fix them.

In further discussing the role of military personnel in the overall PRT work programme, some NZDF personnel also expressed the belief that the governance of the province was beyond the NZDF — again, to reiterate Morris — because personnel did not have specialist training in development. It was felt that it was most useful for NZDF to provide specialist advisors: for example, project managers or legal experts. Despite this, it is also important to note that the MFAT personnel believed that NZDF had done pretty well in contributing to development.

Perceptions of the NZDF efforts

INDEED, DURING THE PERIOD OF the author's visit, there seemed to be a wide belief that the NZDF had done an excellent job in Bamiyan (for more on outsiders' views on the NZDF see the preceding chapter by Greener). The PRT director (MFAT) expressed the views that the NZDF forces were highly competent in their security roles, and that NZDF members were good at operating in a multicultural environment. Indeed, the MFAT personnel appeared to believe that NZDF personnel were generally a lot better than those of other countries at interacting with the local population.

This view was reinforced by civilian and military personnel from other countries. One USAID member noted that the Kiwi soldiers were disciplined but laid-back. He said that the civilian–military integration appeared to work well, and in his view was better than in other militaries. The USAID chief noted that the NZDF personnel seemed very capable and patient. He said that people knew that New Zealand had done the best job in Afghanistan in terms of its PRT being the best integrated with other nations. He felt comfortable dealing with New Zealand commanders as he did not have to play 'ego games' with them. The EUPOL chief noted that the police chief in Sayghan (a town and district to the north) had said that the NZ PRT could stay as long as it wanted.

Additionally, in the author's observation, the NZDF service personnel themselves appeared to be in high spirits and were both highly motivated and professional in their behaviour. The local people responded well to the presence of patrols. Indeed, the drawing down of the PRT was voiced with some concern, with one individual commenting that:

> The PRT is seen as being here for security, to look after the Hazara people. People are starting to come to the realisation we are leaving and putting a survival face on. These have been very good years for the Hazarajat — they have really taken advantage of the opportunities to educate their people. Now they are going into survival mode with some anger and resentment. They are asking, well, what have you done here anyway? The local people see transition as abandonment.

For the most part, then, the NZDF element of the PRT arguably acquitted itself well. A Kiwi contractor working for an international company based in the province suggested that the NZDF were highly knowledgeable, professional, educated and friendly, and that they had a high level of respect for the Afghan people. However, through no fault of the soldiers, this individual suggested that military-to-local interactions were always tense. In explaining why this might be, he noted that soldiers were required to be armed, and this brought a major shift of atmosphere to any meeting. He said that when NZDF soldiers were invited to enter a local meeting room, they were always very polite and courteous, but you could always sense a stiffening of tensions and a cooling of temper in the Afghans. In that sense it would be difficult for any soldier to overcome the 'occupying army' barrier. He noted that, for civilians, an armed military patrol passing by was always scary, and with fear comes resentment. He experienced this in a number of situations when NZDF and US military patrols passed by, noting that each time his emotions would shift from fear to anger. This is also a theme discussed in the chapter by Stevens and Greener, and in Fish et al. (this volume).

Conclusion

FOR ME, THE MOST STRIKING example of the work of the PRT and how it was received by the locals came when I was walking along the Bamiyan bazaar. An elderly gentleman came up and, catching me slightly unawares, grabbed my hand and shook it firmly. He disappeared into the crowd again as quickly as he had appeared. His hand felt incredibly calloused from a lifetime of hard toil, and I can only guess at what he thought of my much softer skin.

I noted the degree of humility that the New Zealand troops displayed in their dealings with the local population, and the genuine interest that they were able to convey. Groups of children continued to play happily as we drove by, and when we walked along the bazaar in Sayghan we were eventually surrounded by kids. However, the situation was not completely black and white. We were occasionally scowled at by locals in Bamiyan town. And, although I did not observe it myself, I have been told of cases where NZDF personnel interacted with the local population in a less than cordial but rather overzealous fashion.

In terms of what readers might take away from this chapter, it is important to note that personnel were keen to be better equipped to acquit themselves in this deployment. Most personnel did not believe that they had been sufficiently prepared to understand the cultural environment and human terrain prior to deployment; nor did they feel capable of properly engaging in development work.

In the end, though, whatever the limitations of the development efforts and the actions of the NZDF, environmental and external factors will eventually have a heavy impact on the shape of the province. The legacy of the PRT will most likely be the memory of genuine efforts over a decade to help local people try to fix a broken situation.

06

The New Zealand Army, Peacekeeping and Masculinities in the Solomon Islands

K. Stevens and B. K. Greener

THIS CHAPTER[1] PICKS UP ON a theme raised in the previous chapter: the consequences of choosing to utilise armed military personnel on peace and stability operations. When new allegations arise about UN peacekeepers' abuse of civilians, such as those currently levelled at peacekeepers in the Central African Republic (Al Jazeera 2016) and Haiti (Code Blue 2016), we might again wonder whether or not good soldiers always make good peacekeepers. Having soldiers act as peacekeepers in the post-conflict development space is not new; yet increasingly soldiers are working multilaterally and interacting closely with local people as mandates have broadened and deepened to encompass peace-building and security sector reform (SSR) efforts. In such interactions, gender sensitivity and cultural awareness are increasingly necessary. Concomitantly, the gendered practices and gendering processes of the military have been a theme for feminists studying questions of security and military involvement in peace-building operations.

Researchers such as Betts Fetherston (1998), Higate and Henry (2004), Whitworth (2004), Higate (2007), Simic (2012), Duncanson (2013), and Neudorfor (2015), amongst others, have highlighted the increase in prostitution, trafficking, sexual harassment and violence present in post-conflict

1. This chapter is solely the work of the authors. Any views expressed in it are those of the authors and do not necessarily represent or reflect official policy of the New Zealand Government or of any government agency.

countries where there are peacekeeping or peace-building operations. A number of these authors argue that the *particular* form of traditional masculinity valued and produced in militaries potentially makes them unsuitable for peacekeeping operations and thus not conducive to creating lasting peace. Such theorists argue that there is an inherent contradiction in having those trained in the tasks that are useful for a soldier in a war-fighting context (violence) undertaking roles that are mainly about building and maintaining peace. Thus it has been argued that:

> There is no switch inside a Blue Helmet that automatically turns a soldier trained for war-fighting into an individual prepared to work non-violently and with cultural sensitivity in a highly militarised environment (Betts Featherston 1998: 159).

These arguments cast doubt on the popular notion that good war-fighters make for good peacekeepers, and even on the notion that 'only soldiers can do it'.

When Secretary General Dag Hammerskjold introduced the concept of peacekeeping to the UN in the 1950s, he argued that although peace-keeping wasn't a soldier's job, only a soldier could do it. The reasoning behind this assertion is simple. Peacekeeping is typically undertaken in a volatile environment that can quickly move from relatively stable to violently hostile. Military personnel, armed with their particular combat skill set, might need to call upon that war-fighting capability in order to respond to serious security challenges arising within the peacekeeping mission in very short time frames.

However, the literature noted above suggests that this argument, though reasonable, neglects to take into account the considerable need for caution in deploying military personnel, given the evolution of peace operations into peace-building work in particular. The values and skills that are said to provide military personnel with the ability to undertake kinetic or war-fighting activities successfully (such as controlled aggression and a willingness to kill) are also the same values and skills that potentially create other risks — particularly for the local civilian population. As the nature of peacekeeping has changed, so, too, have the types of values, tasks and attitudes needed for successful operations.

The critiques made by feminist scholars noted above do not fit obviously with the dominant image of the New Zealand Defence Force (NZDF) — that is, peaceful, culturally sensitive and respectful of women's equality. The NZDF is untarnished by any public international peacekeeping scandal, and, specific to the aims of this research, the Regional Assistance Mission Solomon Islands (RAMSI) mission that it took part in both has largely been considered a success (Glenn 2007; Fepulea'i 2010) and was somewhat demilitarised in terms of its make-up and objectives. The engagement of the NZDF in this mission therefore provides an interesting opportunity to look more closely at concerns about military engagement in peacekeeping.

The nature of this research

THE ORIGINAL RESEARCH SHOWCASED IN this chapter is based mainly on findings from Kiri Stevens' Masterate. This firstly involved undertaking semi-structured interviews in New Zealand with male NZDF personnel, asking for their views on what is valued in undertaking peacekeeping in the Solomon Islands. Secondly, it involved additional fieldwork in the Solomon Islands, where discussions were held with locals in an attempt to better understand their perceptions of the RAMSI mission and of the role of NZDF personnel within it. Where quoted below, these interviewees have been given pseudonyms to ensure their anonymity. The research was therefore predominantly qualitative in approach, seeking to identify common and disparate themes from the discussions and interviews, and then involved engagement by both authors with feminist theorising and analysis of secondary literature on peacekeeping practices. We have consciously incorporated a higher number of references to these feminist sources than in other chapters, as this is an area that is often viewed as quite specialist — ironically so when gender is in fact a significant issue that crosscuts many sites of study.

Essentially this chapter argues that New Zealand Army soldiers both understand, and see value ascribed within the army to, alternative non-violent forms of masculinity. This is significant in the face of the concerns about militarised masculinities expressed above. The practices that soldiers value and consider most useful are constantly changing as a result of their involvement in peacekeeping and other non–war-fighting tasks. Ideas about ideal forms of masculinity are, therefore, this chapter suggests, being engendered at least in part by the need for soldiers to express a sense of equality with, and respect for, local people — the site of entry for our discussion about masculinities and peacekeeping.

The dynamic nature of contemporary soldiering is resulting in the emergence of practices that offer alternatives and/or challenge those hegemonic and racialised, militarised masculinities that have traditionally been valued in the armed forces. Indeed this supports recent research carried out with other modern military forces, such as those in the UK, which suggests an increasing acceptance of a form of 'peacekeeping masculinity' where mutual respect and empathy become core values (Duncanson 2013). And the site for our consideration of this topic is the Regional Assistance Mission to the Solomon Islands.

RAMSI

RAMSI WAS UNPRECEDENTED IN THAT it was a regionally mandated, police-led operation. The first of these factors was necessary in order to ensure legitimacy and buy-in of a range of actors within the South Pacific — without Pacific Island Forum engagement the mission would have been at risk of appearing to be a case of Australian big-brother politics only. The second decision, to place police ahead of military, was made for a number of reasons: there was no ongoing 'war'; the regional force did not want to be seen as an occupying military force; and the relatively low hostility level meant that the environment was permissive enough for this to occur. More significantly, though, this was a mission that — as emphasised in the Facilitation of International Assistance Act (FIAA) 2003, which enabled the mission — required first and foremost a restoration of law and order in the host nation: 'the mission is police-led because addressing the climate of criminality and impunity in Solomon Islands is primarily a policing task' (Wainwright 2003: 493).

Given all of this, the mandate for the military part of the mission — the Combined Task Force (CTF) — was explicitly to act 'in support of' the police.

> To provide protection and support to Participating Police Force (PPF) operations in order to assist the Solomon Islands Police (SIPF) establish and maintain the rule of law in the Solomon Islands (NZ Army 2008).

Military personnel were tasked with securing the environment to a point at which the PPF could begin the task of restoring law and order. The CTF was used in cordon and search operations (Brooke 2005) and to secure the centrally important airport and Camp RAMSI. Army platoons were rotated regularly around the islands, where they undertook patrols with police 'when deemed necessary, albeit in a manner and at a distance designed not to detract from the police operations' (Glenn 2007: 24). Moreover, seven of the 17 police posts established in the first few years were 'accompanied' posts that had a complement of a platoon of soldiers (McDevitt 2006: 10). The CTF was also involved in a wide range of support tasks, including logistics, transport, engineering and the provision of accommodation, catering and emergency medical facilities, including airborne medical evacuation (ibid.: 11).

The purpose of the military component of RAMSI was therefore very much to provide a secure working environment for the police and other civilian actors. Moreover, the mission in its later iterations drew significantly on reserve forces. This sets a scene where the military role is both explicitly acting in a support role to other security providers (the PPF and the SIPF), *and* that support role does not automatically assume that combat is a likely requirement as opposed to a more deterrence-based role.

The RAMSI deployment, then, was not one that emphasised a need for or likelihood of significant aggression or armed conflict — rendering it a somewhat demilitarised mission on the scale of peacekeeping operations and weakening any demands for a more 'militarised masculinity' to be performed.

Militarised masculinities?

THE TERM 'GENDER' IS OFTEN associated in common discourse with 'women'. Examining UN documents on 'gender', for example, demonstrates a tendency to associate the term with women and, from there, to reinforce the notion of women as victims (see the contributions to Sylvester 2011 and the *International Journal of Feminist Politics* Special Issue 13 [4] 2011). In correct usage, however, the term refers to the various feminine and masculine roles, traits and characteristics that may be associated with women or men or transgender individuals.

Gender is thus a term that refers to the social construction of 'men' and 'women' or 'male' and 'female' or 'masculine' or 'feminine': 'to people who study it, gender indicates something about socialized behaviour patterns' (Przygoda and Chrisler 2000: 554). What this means is that the term 'gender' does not refer solely to 'sex' or to those biological properties that assign us a physical type, but, again, to the social roles typically ascribed simply because of our chromosomes or outward physical image. And, importantly, those masculine and feminine traits are valued differently within different societies.

In the Western world, for example, feminist authors claim that 'masculine' traits such as rationality, autonomy, objectivity, competitiveness and aggression are valued more than 'feminist' traits such as emotion, empathy, subjectivity, cooperation and compromise. Men are associated with the former, women with the latter. Moreover, the first set of traits is associated with what is valued in the public sphere and 'high politics', whereas the latter set is associated with what is valued in the private sphere. This has flow-on effects for how we rank the importance of various political issues, for how we understand security, for how we view work and economic life, and for whom we see as authoritative in public life. So gender is a variable that can be used to try to understand what is valued most within society, who is associated with what activities, and why.

In unpacking one of these gender concepts further, masculinity, for example, refers to a 'set of attitudes and practices culturally deemed appropriate to men' (Buchbinder 1994: vii; see also Sjoberg 2013). But masculinity is never set in stone. It is always being negotiated and remade through performing those expected practices (see Butler 1990 on this idea of 'performativity'). Different contexts each have an 'ideal' masculinity (and femininity, though we do not discuss this here), which is celebrated. Men do not necessarily fit that ideal — it is more something that all men are expected to aspire to. If men do not conform, or do not appear to conform, in attempting to achieve this ideal, then they may be discriminated against or find themselves at a disadvantage. In military contexts the traditional warrior soldier (see Derbyshire, this volume), or 'militarised masculinity', has typically been viewed as being the prevalent ideal (Whitworth 2004; Duncanson 2013).

In contexts where 'militarised masculinity' is the ideal, authors such as Whitworth and Duncanson suggest that value is placed on an individual's ability to endure hardship, their capacity for controlled violence, exultation of the bonds between fellow soldiers over all others, commitment to the completion of assigned tasks without complaint, and rationality. Traditionally, moreover, combat and all it brings has been the touchstone for defining ideal masculinities — often within military institutions *and* in other national settings more generally. Cynthia Enloe thus argued in the early 1980s that:

> The notion of combat plays a central role in the construction of notions of manhood and justifications for the superiority of maleness in the social order. In reality, of course, to be a soldier of the state means to be subservient, obedient and almost totally dependent. But that mundane reality is hidden behind a potent myth: to be a soldier means possibly to experience 'combat', and only in combat lies the ultimate test of a man's masculinity (1983: 12).

Yet peacekeeping is not combat. It therefore presents a range of challenges to military institutions that are primarily geared towards war-fighting.

Moreover, radical feminist views on the culture of military forces suggest that the process of becoming a soldier, and indeed being a soldier, may be broadly problematic when those personnel are utilised in a peacekeeping setting. These authors, for example, argue that a dousing of or complete elimination of any femininity or difference in ethnicity or sexuality is needed in order for soldiers to fit comfortably within a highly regulated institution that seeks to break down individuals and then to rebuild them as parts of a military machine (Whitworth 2004). Particular masculine traits are adopted or accentuated in order for this fitting in to occur (see Harding, this volume, for a competing view on this process of making soldiers). The competent use of weapons and controlled aggression, in particular, are important parts of that form of militarised masculinity that equates manliness with the sanctioned use of violence and control. So let us look at what a focus on masculinity as a factor might tell us about the RAMSI mission.

Militarised masculinities at play?

IN THE SOLOMON ISLANDS, THE possession of weapons, particularly by young men, was and is equated with status and power. One of the most important parts of the RAMSI mission was thus an arms amnesty, initiated in the first few days. Local people were encouraged to surrender weapons without any threat of prosecution — though they would face harsh penalties, up to 10 years' imprisonment or a $25,000 fine, if found with weapons after the amnesty expired (McDevitt 2006: 14). This initiative helped RAMSI to collect 3725 weapons in short order (Frankel 2004: 168–9). Military personnel helped with the logistics of the amnesty operations and also stored and destroyed the weapons seized. But they themselves remained armed.

The use of weapons to create peace can be connected to hyper-masculine practices and is problematic in post-conflict environments, where weapons have often been used by militants to challenge existing social structures. A particularly innovative and brave response to this conundrum was aptly demonstrated in an earlier (late 1990s) intervention in Bougainville. Here, following calls for help to find resolution to the Bougainville conflict, New Zealand engaged in a long-term process whereby it provided neutral ground for peace talks and then engaged in a Truce Monitoring Group. This decision to undertake an unarmed monitoring role was novel in approach but deemed necessary at the time to help diminish intimidation and engender trust between the New Zealand Army and the local population (see Adams 2001; Rolfe 2001).

Such less-militarised models of engagement, as well as the use of alternative agents (see Fish et al., this volume), are worth reconsidering in future operations — particularly as the presence of weapons was also consistently raised by locals in the Solomon Islands as a problematic issue. Below, for example, 'James' questions the use of soldiers as it undermines culturally appropriate conflict resolution practices:

> . . . you know, just the sight of them . . . it's intimidating . . . and it also makes the traditional system ineffective . . . In the sense that when . . . anything [is] happening in the villages, 'Oh, I know tellim RAMSI will come'; 'we will call RAMSI'. So I mean [they are] now talking about streamlining [an] exit strategy, so we come back to where we were . . . for me one of the most important things is to empower . . . the traditional system in the villages and communities, yeah . . . Like it's just a mentality that people have, like when [someone] have a gun one have the power here, like you, you're the hero. Yeah, so you have the power. So this guy, the chief and the elder in the village does not have the power. So to me I interpret that as an intimidation . . . Just the sight of it . . . you know, when we had the ethnic tension, I'm a school teacher and you see the small children that you are teaching in classroom some few years ago, [now] carrying guns . . . They can press the trigger any time, I mean, yeah, so . . . this kind of mentality lingers on, like you see people carrying [a] gun and then when the soldiers come, the only difference is they have their uniform.

For James, the use of guns by RAMSI soldiers, and the threat of violence implicit in this, was no different from the behaviour of those who had caused the issues in the first place: the militants who had prompted the 'troubles' in which death, kidnapping and intimidation were utilised as tactics by all sides in the conflict (Frankel 2004). The only difference from his perspective was that the RAMSI soldiers were wearing uniforms. This was picked up on by NZDF personnel.

Although appearing strong and acting aggressively was recognised as an important aspect of being a soldier, when describing the training for the 'hearts and minds' approach needed for RAMSI, 'Henry' (a member of the NZDF) also stated that their intention was not to appear aggressive:

> Reinforcing the fact that we were there, we're not there with an aggressive posture, there is no enemy as such, as a normal soldier would be trained, yeah, you were there to engage and impress and . . . interact with the population in a very friendly way.

In the peacekeeping process, alternative qualities such as being empathetic, not being inclined to use violence to solve problems and seeing the importance of building friendships (such as chatting with locals) are valued as useful. These qualities are often designated as being inherently feminine in nature. Importantly, then, such qualities were also understood as having significant value in peace-building missions by members of the NZDF interviewed for this research, and as having an impact on accepted masculinities.

For example, 'Steve', another member of the NZDF, articulates an admiration for another soldier who embodied a more militarised masculinity while simultaneously recognising that this was not necessarily conducive to the success of the RAMSI mission:

> Another guy I worked with in the field of intelligence — he was senior NCO, he was just hard out war-y, like he'd been to Afghanistan and seconded to the marines to train American marines in Afghanistan; he'd a been a sniper, a recon soldier, and an intelligence operator; and [he] . . . oozed that military confidence. But that would be more beneficial in a conventional warfare environment.

Noting that although this experience afforded the individual the confidence to then 'get shit done', Steve wasn't entirely sure that the overall demeanour was appropriate for the tasks at hand.

Such dominant gendered expectations still exist within the NZDF to a certain degree. Here, for example, is 'Henry' again, on being a good soldier with traditional militarised masculinities:

> It turned out our females weren't all that great unfortunately [laughs], which I mean . . . I don't mean to sound sexist but they really sucked [laughs] . . . they weren't particularly good soldiers, I mean . . . not particularly good with weapons systems, carrying packs, getting by without any sleep; one of them was much better than the other one but she sort of withdrew into herself and stopped interacting with the section and that kind of played with the dynamics. Yeah, and the other one got really homesick and stopped eating and things — it was quite worrying.

Such an attitude implies that being a good soldier was first of all associated with the skills of being good with weapons systems, despite the fact that these personnel were deployed in an environment that was relatively permissible, and despite the professed need to carefully consider the role of aggression in building trust. It shows, too, the contradictions soldiers face when thinking about their role on deployment. To a certain extent 'Steve' and 'Henry' challenged and reworked militarised forms of masculinity by also valuing skills that have typically been associated with femininity and alternative forms of masculinity. Understanding these contradictions in the narrative is important for understanding how gender roles, such as those associated with masculinity, are created and recreated.

Undertaking a gendered analysis

BY USING GENDER ANALYSIS TO focus on what was happening for individual soldiers on the ground in the Solomon Islands, we began to identify contradictions in the narratives that NZDF personnel told about their identity, tasks and values as soldiers in a peace-building context. This would indicate that the masculinities that soldiers value, and to which they aspire, change in response to the skills required of a peacekeeping force.

Soldiers value and understand the need for skills that are most effective for bringing about peace in the Solomon Islands context, but at the same time they still value the more 'masculine' aspects of the defence forces — particularly the importance of war-fighting skills (again, see Derbyshire, this volume). This may seem obvious given that the core task of the NZDF is the 'defence of New Zealand', but many tasks assigned to the NZDF no longer have war-fighting elements.

When we consider some of the Solomon Islanders' reflections on the RAMSI deployment, for some participants it was the soldiers' behaviours that can be linked with femininity and alternative masculine practices that were the most positively received. These practices included: valuing the need for cross-cultural relationship-building through communication skills, demonstrating empathy, respect for local cultural practices and a willingness to be flexible. For example, 'Ronnie', another local, compliments aspects of a New Zealand soldier's behaviour that are linked to non-hegemonic masculinities:

> When they were in the village while this man [the leader of RAMSI] was giving a talk, like he [another soldier] is engaging with the people in the village, talking and communicating, like discussing and things, yeah . . . it's very, very approachable in a sense, yeah, people come up and ask him questions and things.

Similarly, 'Andrew', another Solomon Islander, is even more explicit about valuing soldiers who do not act in a macho way:

> Sometimes it's good to demonstrate masculinity but sometimes it's not so necessary. I think when . . . you respect and you go down and uphold the weak part of society, that has more impact, is more realistic and has a lasting . . . memory within a society . . . [whereas] if you're a military officer a lieutenant or a sergeant . . . [and] you go in the village and you like [indicates a tough stance] you know, no. But when you go and say hello and you shake hands and they offer you something and you receive it, that has more respect . . . lasting respect.

This view may be validated by the fact that during the deployment to the Solomon Islands, the NZDF's presence was a deterrent to any further conflict. Military personnel engaged in a variety of tasks such as travelling around and talking with locals with the aim of providing this sense of 'security', attempting to maintain a clear distinction from policing duties. The skills necessary to accomplish these tasks included the ability to be friendly and chat informally, taking into account cross-cultural differences and communication skills such as relationship-building and negotiation (see Wineera and P. Greener, this volume). Though some may see these as gender-neutral skill sets, these are those sorts of traits that are associated with subjectivity and empathy — principles typically associated with femininity.

Gender as a variable is relevant in this context, given that such skills are not merely to do with competence or expedience but are also seen to be inherently 'feminine', thereby rendering the motivation for and successful uptake of such skills potentially difficult within an institutional setting that also values particularly militarised forms of masculinity. Moreover, while gender considerations are emphasised in much of development practice, any lack of significant gender training for soldiers (see Derbyshire, this volume) — gender training that could contribute positively to the impact that their presence may have — is potentially damaging, particularly for non-violent conflict resolutions in the post-conflict space.

What a focus on gender might bring to the table

A LACK OF COMPREHENSIVE GENDER training is even more precarious in strikingly different social environments such as Afghanistan, where soldiers are unable to rely on any possible similarities in Pacific cultures to understand the gendered implications of their practices. However, we must note not only that gender norms are quite varied across the Pacific (indeed, there are a number of groups that prioritise matrilineal lines in Melanesia in particular), but also that in its pre-deployment training for both Afghanistan and Iraq the NZDF has increasingly emphasised the need for cultural awareness (see Wineera, this volume). Some of the skill sets noted above that are often associated more with feminine values, then, are becoming more central.

Gender training also illuminates certain other dynamics at play. First of all it highlights the operational significance and importance of recruiting and deploying more women personnel for peacekeeping missions, given that women can at times more easily undertake particular roles within those missions (Bennett 2009; Bridges and Horsfall 2009). It also helps to rectify gender bias in the form of assumed attitudes towards women and men.

For example, as Charlesworth (2008) has noted, the wider assumptions of RAMSI personnel about the 'traditional role' of women in the Solomon Islands as being reticent meant that women were excluded from peace processes. Thus, in the context of soldiers' everyday engagements with local people, a failure to talk to women, or approach them in a way that suggested that they held any power, reinforced their exclusion from gaining respect and equality in post-conflict Solomon Islands. This is a significant oversight given that, just as in the case of Bougainville noted earlier, women were both implicated in initiating conflict and instrumental in attempts to bring peace. For example, Higgins notes that 'the process of resolving conflicts and keeping the peace in communities . . . in many societies (at least throughout Malaita and Temotu) . . . was traditionally the role of the mature woman' (2008: 4; see also Leslie 2002; Paina 2000; Pollard 2000).

The overlooking of the actual or potential role of women is an issue not limited to RAMSI. As then UN Secretary General Kofi Annan observed:

> We can no longer afford to minimize or ignore the contributions of women and girls to all stages of conflict resolution, peacemaking, peace-building, peacekeeping and reconstruction processes. Sustainable peace will not be achieved without the full and equal participation of women and men (UN 2005b: front cover).

Indeed, recent research suggests that one of the few reliable indicators for the likelihood of a country being peaceable is levels of gender equality (Hudson 2012), while a similar indicator for the likelihood of sustainable success for peacemaking efforts is whether or not women's groups have been engaged in the process (Accord Insight 2013).

On the opposite side of the coin, many women who were also combatants have been left out of disarmament, demobilisation and reintegration (DDR) programmes because pacific roles have been assumed (McKenzie 2009; Mobekk 2010) — and anecdotal evidence points to a similar situation in RAMSI with regard to women instigating violent conflict, if not carrying it out (Greener, Fish and Tekulu 2011). Preconceptions and bias around gender roles can foster the unthinking assumption that women are to be considered non-combatants. As Higate and Henry (2004: 490) point out, a more militarised masculinity potentially feeds assumptions in discourses of peacekeepers as 'saviours of the war-torn citizenry' where it becomes inevitable that women require men's protection. These tropes can unhelpfully reinforce stereotypical notions of women as victims, as lacking political and social power, and as non-complicit in conflict and crime.

Recognition of gender as a more fluid social construct, training in terms of the possible particular needs of men and women in peace and stability missions, and an awareness of the need to comprehend the social roles ascribed to men and women in different societies are therefore valuable potential military 'tools' that add to the professional skill set of personnel. This means that gender training and a facilitation of alternative views on masculinity and femininity are not at all in conflict with the modern emphasis on professionalism, but indeed instead add significantly to that objective.

Integrating a gender perspective also opens up the possibility of attempting to ascertain what is genuinely useful in the contexts in which the soldiers are operating, and ensuring that the training is appropriate — even if this is not in the 'war-y hard-out' tradition of old. 'Doing gender' comprehensively, then, can mean much more than just talking nicely to women, or equalising gender ratios. It means asking what it is that we as New Zealanders value and why, how relationships work, and where sites of power lie (for more on this type of feminist approach to undertaking study see Ackerly, Stern and True 2006).

Conclusion

IF WE UNDERSTAND GENDER AS relational, then how we understand, embody and value masculinities also has a relational impact on how we value femininities and those who express values seen to be feminine. We know that gender equality is important in post-conflict development policy, and this has most often translated into a focus on increasing the inclusion of women in peacekeeping forces and in local peace-building processes. This has meant that men are most often typecast as the perpetrators of violence despite evidence, in contemporary development contexts, that this is not always the case. This in turn means that we are failing to recognise, value and support non-violent masculinities that are important to the creation of long-term peace, and important for the support of women's equality.

'Steve' and 'Henry's' experiences and understandings of peacekeeping demonstrate that, contrary to some feminist discourses on militarised masculinity, soldiers are not monolithically violence-oriented when conflict resolution is necessary. This may, in part, be due to the fact that militarised masculinity is tempered both by individual experiences (Higate and Henry 2004) and by national ideologies. A 2008 study on the UN Mission in Liberia suggested that:

> national contingent identity shaped participant understandings of the gendered styles of peacekeepers' security practices to which they were subject. Here, Nigerian troops of the previous ECOMOG presence were seen as 'hard men', Bangladeshi troops were considered as somewhat 'weak' or 'soft' and Swedish and Irish contingent personnel were framed as 'fair' and 'professional' . . . [thus] different styles of peacekeeping articulated at a national level find expression 'on-the-ground', as they converge with national stereotypes held by participants (Sanghera, Henry and Higate 2008: 3).

As the NZDF negotiates how it conceives of its own identity and expressions of its national feminine and masculine values, the emphasis on professionalism noted elsewhere in this book may not only come to mean that it is levels of professionalism rather than levels of masculinity that denote competency, but also that being a professional soldier requires a much stronger awareness of broader gender issues as a whole, and that soldiering itself becomes a stronger mix of traits associated with both femininity and masculinity.

These changes are arguably part of a broader trend worldwide. In the private security industry, for example, Higate (2015) observed, when undertaking participant observation in training for close protection roles, that many UK and US companies are today utilising the binary of the undesirable 'hypermasculine' versus the more desirable 'professional' private security contractor — noting the use of the phrase 'Don't be a Billy Big-Bollocks' as indicative of these changing attitudes.

And soldiers' practices do change in response to the changing nature of soldiering. This is recognised both by the novel approach of previous engagements in Bougainville and in the new New Zealand Defence White Paper (Ministry of Defence 2016a), which calls for soldiers to both be 'combat ready' and 'be able to build trust, negotiate, reduce tension in volatile situations and cope well with ambiguity' (55), as well as in the changes in training approaches noted by Wineera (this volume). Harding's emphasis on soldiering being about competence, and Morris's emphasis on soldiers being willing, albeit not trained fully, to undertake development roles (again this volume), suggest that a consideration of gender issues may have a useful role in redefining competency and professionalism. The need for soldiers to create security by engaging in practices that focus on culturally appropriate, equal communication and relationship-building is therefore engendering new ideas about masculinity in the military.

In bringing this discussion back to the case of RAMSI, we would remind the reader that the process of militarisation is the privileging of military solutions over all other avenues of action. The presence of armed peacekeepers at the cessation of conflict reinforces and disciplines Solomon Islanders in such a way that conflict resolution practices that are non-violent (and most often associated with femininity) are potentially ignored or not valued so highly. As Myrttinen (2009) notes, 'given the delicate nature of peacekeeping operations . . . overt displays of militarised masculinity may end up backfiring, intimidating and alienating the local population'.

Thus, regardless of soldiers' ability to engage with local residents in ways that build positive relationships of trust and demonstrate a sense of equality at an everyday level, in conflicts such as that in the Solomon Islands, where the prevalence of weapons was important for determining who held power, the carrying of weapons by soldiers bears an underlying message about appropriate ways to resolve conflict. Moreover, the recent stories about peacekeepers embroiled in accusations of abuse noted at the beginning of this chapter involve countries whose cultural mores are similar to New Zealand's — French and Canadian troops have been caught up in these recent scandals, not just 'others' from developing countries. As more New Zealand soldiers become involved in post-conflict development space as peacekeepers, we need to keep asking these questions about the role they have in this space (see again Fish et al., this volume) and how questions related to gender, power and expected social roles affect this engagement, so as to keep both soldiers and citizens safe.

New Zealand soldiers and Solomon Islanders.

07

Women in the Armed Forces

Lieutenant Colonel Jane Derbyshire

CURRENTLY, THERE IS NO COUNTRY in the world where women are equal to men. This is in terms of all areas of livelihood, economic security, political rights and personal safety (Miller, Pournik and Swaine 2014). However, the aim of gender equality is being progressed in many countries and New Zealand has a long history of being a leader in promoting the rights of women. New Zealand was the first self-governing country in the world to grant universal suffrage to women, in 1893; it has a comprehensive set of legislation intended to protect human rights and eliminate discrimination against women and it consistently ranks at the top of global indices measuring equality of opportunity for women (MFAT 2015a: 10).

Unsurprisingly, then, the New Zealand Defence Force (NZDF) is a leader in gender equity compared with many other militaries in the world. All restrictions to New Zealand women serving in combat roles were formally removed in 2000 (MFAT 2015a: 6), and the NZDF has had a higher female representation in the regular forces than the US, Australia, Canada or the UK (MoD 2014b: 3). Other militaries have therefore looked to New Zealand as a model for integrating women into existing combat corps (ibid.: 11). Moreover, even before the law was formally changed in the Human Rights (Women in Armed Forces) Amendment Act 2007 to prevent any discrimination on the basis of sex, the first women were posted onto navy ships in 1986, and in 1988 the air force opened up all roles to women.

Given all of this, some may say that there is no problem with the current role of women in the NZDF. However, in a Ministry of Defence Equity Review published in 2014, the NZDF officially recognised that little progress had been made in increasing the total percentage of women employed by the services, and, in fact, that representation in the last five years had been falling (MoD 2014b: 3). In a subsequent press release in 2014, the Chief of Defence Force (CDF) Lieutenant General Tim Keating said that the NZDF 'should not be content with simply doing better than those [comparable] countries', that the NZDF was 'missing out on a significant pool of talent in our community' and that 'we know that women have been a significant success factor in the missions we have undertaken over the past decade' (Keating cited in MoD 2014a).

This chapter outlines the current position of women in the NZDF and examines the challenges faced in recruiting and retaining women within the organisation. It begins from a personal point of view, then moves on to examine a range of external and internal factors, such as societal influences and the organisational and strategic culture of the NZDF. It discusses the importance of women globally, peace and security imperatives, and identifies key opportunities for meaningfully incorporating women in creating a sustainable peace. The chapter argues that New Zealand and the NZDF need to further redefine the identity of the modern warrior, already discussed to some degree in the preceding chapters, in light of gender-based arguments, in order to be fully effective in our contemporary environment.

A woman in the armed forces

MY PARTNER AND I ARE in the military and have been all our working lives. We both aspire for our son and daughter to believe that every option is open for them in the world and we strive not to gender-stereotype their, or our, behaviour. Last year my daughter was in her first year of primary school, and Anzac Day commemorations were held and discussed. We also took the children to a memorial service where they saw us wear both our own and our grandparents' medals, whose significance we took some time to explain. My daughter had a lot of Anzac Day-related questions over the next few months. One day she asked me if Daddy was going to die in war because he was a soldier. I spent some time talking this over with her honestly and sensitively. She seemed satisfied and quietly went back to her drawing. So I asked, 'You know that Mummy is a soldier too, don't you, sweetheart?' With that she gave a loud laugh and said, 'Don't be silly, Mummy,' and went back to drawing. I then explained that she had seen Mummy and Daddy wearing the same uniform going to work each day, and that she had seen Mummy's medals on Anzac Day. 'Mummy is a soldier too,' I concluded. She replied, 'Don't be silly, Mummy, girls can't be soldiers!' She certainly hadn't learned that from her parents. I hope that this chapter provides some reasons why this belief, that girls can't be soldiers, persists in our children and our society today.

Women in the armed forces

THE CORE PURPOSE OF THE NZDF is to prepare for combat (Keating, cited in State Services Commission Review 2015: 3). Historically, symbolically and numerically the NZDF is a male-dominated organisation. The military has been one of the last bastions of male occupational monopoly, and it is not disputed that as an organisation it has a masculine brand that is, stereotypically, going to appeal more to men. Therefore, some may conclude that the current percentage of women simply represents the nature of the profession, but this is an overly simplistic rendering of the issue.

One of the first formal considerations of women in the armed forces, the Report of the Gender Integration Audit of the NZDF (also known as the 'Burton Report'), was published in 1999. The report's authors found significant evidence of widespread gender harassment, a lack of family-friendly policies and an overall lack of acceptance of women in military roles. Fifteen years later, the Ministry of Defence published a study titled *Maximising Opportunities for Military Women in the New Zealand Defence Force* (also known as the 'Equity Review'). The aim of this review was to explore to what degree regular force (full-time) women in the NZDF are 1) treated equitably, 2) able to achieve their full potential and 3) safe from harassment, bullying and assault (MoD 2014b).

The Equity Review found that there had been substantial progress towards gender equity since the Burton Report. It confirmed, for example, that the NZDF had higher levels of representation of women in the regular forces compared with the US, Australia, Canada or the UK. However, it also found that there was still much more to be done, particularly with respect to recruitment, retention and progression through to more senior ranks. The executive summary states that 'getting women in the door, into the branches that lead to the most progression opportunities, and retaining them are the biggest challenges for the future' (3).

In particular, the Equity Review stated that:

> 'Credible operational command' is perceived by many as being essential for the Chief of Defence Force role and to date this experience has been provided only by leading in combat/ operations branches (4).

At the time of the report 6 per cent of officers in combat corps/ operations branches were women. The Equity Review found that under-representation in these branches, in particular, resulted in limited career progression opportunities for women. Further, it found that small improvements in retention can make a big difference in total representation (14).

The Equity Review concluded that while there are no longer formal restrictions on women joining the combat/operational branches, the legacy of historical limitations remains. Further, that in order to be the

CDF it is perceived that you 'need to be a warrior' from a combat corps/ operational branch. Thus, it is hoped, if women gain representation in those branches then that will increase their opportunities for progression to the top (28–9). The report made four recommendations:

1. Recruit the best personnel, by focusing on a broader potential candidate pool.
2. Expand systems to increase women's retention.
3. Improve pathways for women to attain senior leadership roles.
4. Further reduce discrimination, harassment and bullying, particularly in recruit training.

By the time of its publication in 2014 some of the Equity Review's concerns had already been raised and targeted by the CDF. Concerns around women having been and still being under-represented in the military had led the CDF to create the NZDF Women's Development Steering Group (WDSG) in 2013 (HQNZDF CDF Minute 2013). The WDSG's objectives are to promote the operational effectiveness of the NZDF by means of an integrated and diverse total workforce, and progress key NZDF Strategic Initiative M9 (recruit and retain the right people) by promotion of developmental opportunities for women. There are also single-service groups that promote similar objectives within their service.

As at June 2016, three years after the initiation of the WDSG and two years after the publication of the Equity Review, the percentage of women in the armed forces has increased by 1 per cent (MoD 2016a: 82). The navy has the highest percentage with 21 per cent, then the air force with 18 per cent and army with 13 per cent (ibid.: 83–6). In particular, there are only 27 women currently serving in the combat and combat support corps (Infantry [RNZIR], Artillery [RNZA], Armoured [RNZAC], Engineers [RNZE]) in the army (NZDF 2016c). As of yet no women have served as badged SAS members. More needs to be done, but there are a number of challenges to overcome.

Challenges and opportunities

COMMON ARGUMENTS PRESENTED AGAINST THE inclusion of women in defence forces are that: women aren't physically capable, therefore standards would need to be lowered (Marine General Kelly cited in Seck 2016); men may try to protect women on the battlefield; the likelihood of public revulsion over battlefield deaths increases political risk; women lack the aggression needed for close combat (Kemp 2014); admitting women into previously all-male units has a negative impact on unit cohesion and morale; women may not be culturally accepted by the local population; a woman might be raped; women undertaking the roles will lower the social prestige (van Creveld 2000); and there isn't suitable accommodation. Some of these concerns are discussed in more detail below, followed by a consideration of the benefits of gender mainstreaming.

There are overly paternalistic and protectionist concerns about women's physical ability, and small-minded concerns about the necessity of separate accommodation. However, some women are already displaying their ability to perform the physical role required (Lemmon 2015), and professional units increasingly live together and fight together (Kremer 2013). Some years ago Joshua Goldstein (2001) demonstrated that a very fit woman can easily physically outperform an average man. Thus, he asserted, although there are small, innate biological gender differences in average size and strength, this is not a reason to exclude those women who are physically capable. Lowering job-specific required standards to accommodate all women would be a failure, as, just as General Ann Dunwoody, the first female US four-star general, stated:

> I think it is smart the Army and the military are methodically looking at each one of these branches and career fields to determine what the standard is. They can't lower those standards, once identified, to accommodate women coming into those fields. That would

> be a failure. We're not a social experiment. We're a war fighting institution, and that's dangerous business (cited in Tan 2015).

Instead, increased efforts have usefully gone into reviewing fitness standards based on objective assessments of combat requirements on the modern battlefield (Egnell 2013: 35).

Aside from arguments of a physical nature, there are other arguments that suggest women should be excluded from a deployment owing to the perceptions of another culture, usually the host nations, and their acceptance of women. However, some respond by suggesting that the respect for 'culture' shown by the international community can often be based on a monolithic view of culture; the view being that the culture has 'no internal diversity and no potential for a critical tradition or a commitment to human rights' (Sunder cited in Chinkin and Charlesworth 2006: 945). Women's groups in Iraq and Afghanistan are pioneering change for local women, and world leaders in gender equity should be cognisant of this internal diversity in their own culture. Deploying women inspires a culture of inclusion for the next generation (Inclusive Security 2015) and provides role models for the local population rather than reinforcing gender inequity (Bridges and Horsfall 2009: 122).

Gender equality is, moreover, increasingly recognised as a 'necessary precondition for peace, security and a prosperous society' (Haq in Pring 1999), and there are more tangible results for human security when the root cause of the issue is addressed (UN Trust Fund for Human Security 2014). Therefore, in order to bring about lasting peace, challenging gender stereotypes can be fundamental, and women as peacekeepers can assist with this objective (Austrian Development Cooperation 2009; Sharp 2013; Karim and Beardsley 2013).

Gender mainstreaming is at the heart of the UNSCR 1325 Resolution, discussed later in this chapter, and key to its implementation success (Swaine 2009). The United Nations' Economic and Social Council

(ECOSOC) has a useful definition of gender mainstreaming as 'the process of assessing the implications for women and men of any planned action, including legislation, policies, or programmes, in all areas and all levels' (UN Women n.d.). Gender mainstreaming is widely viewed to be essential in order to achieve transformative change in the women, peace and security agenda. One of NATO/EADC's key outcomes in its national action plan (NAP) for UNSCR 1325 (of which New Zealand is considered a partner) is 'increased operational effectiveness through a gender perspective included in conflict analysis, planning, execution, assessment and evaluation of any NATO-led operations and missions' (NATO 2014). In considering the benefits of gender mainstreaming, then, we can begin within military forces themselves. One core reason for moves within military forces to accept gender equity or mainstreaming policies is the fact that any organisation wants to have the best people working for it, and therefore should attract and recruit personnel from the entire talent pool. On this very point, the Chief of Defence Force said, 'I want to attract and retain the best individuals for leadership and future capability' (Keating cited in *Air Force News* 178[2016]: 15). The Equity Review further noted the benefits arising from the meaningful participation of both genders. These include: increased capability, reduced costs, demonstration of leadership, reduced risks, getting the best performance out of human capital resources, and fully aligning behaviour with values.

Diversity in the workplace in general has a long list of advantages, such as increased creativity, increased productivity, new attitudes, global understanding, new processes, improved decision-making through alternative views being considered and new solutions to difficult problems (Starren, Luijters, Drupsteen, Vilevicius and Eeckelaert 2013; Holvino, Ferdman and Merrill-Sands 2004). Further, as workforce demographics shift and globalisation increases competition for labour resources, diversity becomes a practical necessity in order to generate and sustain people capability. Through capitalising on diversity, the NZDF will be better equipped to respond to any challenge with the right mix of individuals, skills and capabilities. The NZDF is a 'Force for New Zealand', and it is important to represent the New Zealand it serves to protect.

More specifically for modern military forces, the meaningful inclusion of women as peacekeepers, in addition to providing opportunities to display positive role models as noted above, has been recognised as enhancing operational effectiveness (Bridges and Horsfall 2009). Female peacekeepers are said to have an operational advantage over men in specific issues, such as conducting personal searches of women, particularly women combatants at disarmament, demobilisation and reintegration sites (Karim and Beardsley 2013). Moreover, in some nations it is culturally appropriate for women only to speak with women, and female personnel are therefore important given that they can work with the often-neglected 50 per cent of the population, especially in providing support to those women and children who have been victims of gender-based violence (ibid.; Bridges and Horsfall 2009).

Female or mixed engagement teams can also enhance operational effectiveness by being utilised in gathering information, gaining access to local women as a source of that information, and helping to build additional bridges between organisations (Egnell 2013). Research has more generally demonstrated that 'a greater proportion of female military personnel engenders trust and improves the reputations of peacekeepers among local populations' (Bridges and Horsfall 2009). This may be in part because the higher deployment of women may help to decrease the propensity for male peacekeepers to sexually abuse the civilian population. Issues of this nature have increasingly been recognised worldwide and have been further supported by the rise of the 'women, peace and security' (WPS) agenda in international affairs.

Women, peace and security

WITH THE SHIFT AWAY FROM state-centric notions of security towards an awareness and acceptance that human security is central to the future of humankind, it has also been recognised that women and the achievement of peace and security (the WPS agenda) are inextricably interlinked. Women are disproportionately affected by conflict situations and face multiple challenges to their human security. The key starting point for the WPS agenda is that if women fully participate and are equally represented in all aspects of peace-building, peacemaking and peacekeeping, then this will result in a more sustainable peace and fewer conflicts. Such sentiments have, moreover, been expressed formally through the adoption of a number of UN Security Council (UNSC) resolutions.

In 2000, the UNSC passed Resolution 1325. This was the first time that women were officially linked to peace and security within a UN resolution. UNSCR 1325 was the result of a long historical and political process; it had its roots in the UN charter that recognises the equal rights of men and women (Olsson and Gizelis 2013). Since this resolution, seven additional resolutions on WPS have been passed: 1820 (in 2008); 1888 (2009); 1889 (2009); 1960 (2010); 2106 (2013); 2122 (2013) and 2242 (2015). Together these resolutions reaffirm UNSCR 1325 and set the WPS agenda. UNSCR 1325 and subsequent resolutions demand a refocus on viewing women as agents of change, and agents of peace in leadership and decision-making positions, rather than only as victims of war. Women comprise over half of the global population, and yet they remain marginalised and excluded in all aspects of peace and conflict processes (Willett 2010).

UNSCR 1325 called for: an increase in the participation of women at all levels of decision-making; the protection of women from sexual and gender-based violence; the prevention of violence against women through the promotion of women's rights; and the mainstreaming of a gender perspective in all aspects of peace operations (UNSC 2000). It also calls upon countries and regional organisations to develop NAPs to implement UNSCR 1325 and the WPS agenda. New Zealand approved an NAP in October 2015 (MFAT 2015b); the impact of doing so is yet to be realised. UNSCR 1325 didn't just ask governments to simply acknowledge women's important contributions — it also charged them to act. Over 15 years on, however, we are still asking: Where are all the women?

Implementation of UNSCR 1325, most commentators agree, has not yet been successful. Changes are required in order to move from rhetoric to action and then impact. Two areas that are key in the WPS agenda, yet have shown the least progress since UNSCR 1325 was adopted, are the inclusion of women in peace negotiations and as peacekeepers on peacekeeping operations (Miller, Pournik and Swaine 2014). UN gender statistics currently count 4268 women deployed in peacekeeping missions (UN 2016) — accounting for only 4 per cent of peacekeepers. This underscores the fact that there has been no significant increase in the number of women involved in peace negotiations since UNSCR 1325 was passed (Westendorf 2013). Indeed a 2010 UNIFEM (UN Development Fund for Women) report noted that 'women's participation in peace processes remains one of the least well-implemented elements of the women, peace and security agenda' (UNIFEM 2010, cited in Sharp 2013: 160).

To bring about lasting peace and sustainable social development 'there is a need to change the deep-rooted social and cultural conditions that give rise to sexism, racism, authoritarianism, hierarchies and gender stereotypes' (Austrian Development Cooperation 2009). The international community and civil society need to increase the visibility of women, and not just in stereotypical roles. Only with a dual policy approach of the mutually reinforcing pillars of protection and empowerment will the security and status of women improve significantly. Given all of this, then, it is important to consider how to mitigate or help overcome barriers to women's involvement in militaries such as the NZDF — and, as in most countries, some of these barriers are embedded in broader society at large.

Societal influences

THE STATUS OF GENDER EQUITY in New Zealand necessarily influences decisions within the NZDF. New Zealand has a proud history of international leadership in promoting gender equality (MFAT 2015a: 6). However, the Faultlines report of 2015, which was a three-year study of the six major human rights treaties New Zealand has signed, recommends that the New Zealand government take urgent remedial action to retain its point of difference as a human rights leader. One of the issues to address is that of gender equality — with New Zealand having slipped down the gender equality rankings from a typical fifth-to-seventh place over 2006–13 to thirteenth in 2014 (Ryan 2014) before pulling back up to tenth in 2015 (MFAT 2015a).

The military is in many ways a microcosm of society, and prejudices about gender stereotypes are already embedded in individuals before joining (Davidson 1999: 130). The socialisation of children into these gender roles helps reproduce sexist beliefs, with movies, stories and fairy tales planting influential seeds in the minds of children (Boesveld 2014). As children grow up and determine their aspirations for the world, these concepts become their reality in the jobs that they choose (Neikirk 2009; Green 2012). It is notable, then, that our most popular fairy tales, such as *Cinderella* or *Snow White*, perpetuate gender stereotypes with hypermasculine hero men while objectifying and subordinating women who are rewarded for their submissiveness and beauty (Nanda 2014). Recent media and film role models such as Mulan (who joins the army and receives many accolades for bravery [Green 2012]) have begun to challenge these stereotypes, but society remains replete with strictly gendered roles (for more on performing gender, see Butler 1990).

While the culture of the NZDF is strongly influenced by New Zealand society, given that that is from where the majority of its all-volunteer members are drawn, the NZDF is under-representative of society in both ethnicity and gender diversity. This may reflect the idea that New Zealand society has not fully embraced the concept that the modern warrior can be from either gender or any race. Therefore, those entering the NZDF from society may bring their conscious, or unconscious, biases and expectations with them.

National identity and societal influences result in issues for women choosing to participate in the armed forces. In order for women to be considered for all roles for deployments, then, there must be an increase in the recruitment and retention of women, and particularly in combat roles. If women are increasingly represented in the branches that provide 'credible operational command', then they will improve opportunities for women to progress to the higher echelons; currently the highest rank attained by a woman in the NZDF is that of brigadier. The highest-ranked military woman currently serving is a colonel. As Marie Wilson, founder of the White House Project, once famously said, 'You can't be what you can't see.'

There is a growing need to recruit and retain the best skills and talent to the NZDF, and competition for labour talent in the market is strong. The NZDF has acknowledged that the number of women joining the military has dropped to 'disturbing' levels (Gulliver 2015). It is internationally recognised that militaries find it hard to recruit women into what is essentially a very masculine brand, and that negative publicity about sexual harassment of female service members increases the perception that women are not 'wanted in the military and at risk by virtue of their gender' (Avery and McKay 2006). The MoD Equity Review found that the perception in the civilian world is often that women are not truly accepted in the NZDF, and that mums, dads, teachers and friends are important in influencing whether someone will join the military. Therefore, public opinion of the NZDF and gender roles is very important (MoD 2014b), and society plays an important role in discouraging the recruitment of women into the NZDF. One way to address this is to ensure that the organisational culture of the institution does nothing to feed the perception that women are not fully accepted.

Organisational and strategic culture

DESPITE BEING INFLUENCED BY THE society within which it is based, the NZDF also necessarily has a unique culture, distinct from that of society, given that its people must be prepared and willing to fight, and perhaps die, for their country. To meet its purpose, the NZDF cultivates a warrior culture, derived from its history, heritage and experiences of war (NZ Army 2013; see also Morris, this volume). The deep assumptions of this culture include the loyalty, commitment and honour of serving one's country. The ethos, the distinct character of the culture, is based on the concept of service, and is values-based. A previous Chief of Army, Major General Dave Gawn, identified that the culture of the army was forged in historical battles, and noted that historically and culturally 'men fight men in order to defend their values', and that men fight to protect women in society (cited in *Army News* 2015: 3). Although this approach has been perceived as noble, it also reaffirms the essentialist gendered stereotype of men as protectors and women as protected (Willett 2010; Nantais and Lee 1999). Decisions in such institutions are derived at least in part from strategic culture (Kilcullen 2007: 47), and this internal NZDF culture — particularly the emphasis on a warrior culture — may have an unconscious gender bias (Genat et al., 2014; Stevens and Greener, this volume).

Official NZDF doctrine asserts that the modern New Zealand warrior is primarily influenced by the warrior cultures of the Māori and the British (NZDF 2012: 10). This blended warrior concept was recently echoed by the current Chief of Army, Major General Peter Kelly, who stated that he believed he was born into combat with Irish combatants on one side and a Ngāti Toa warrior on the other (Martin 2015: 5). Members of the army are all a part of the tribe of the Māori War God — Ngāti Tūmatauenga — a kinship that is intended to provide unity. A further deep assumption of the NZDF's culture is that history is an important source of learning, inspiration and connectedness, and that this provides the soldier's sense of belonging and identity.

Drilling down further, the legend of Anzac is a particularly important influence on the NZDF warrior culture (as noted in Morris's chapter, this volume). National sentiment is particularly strong with the recent 100-year commemorations. However, the Anzac legend has been described as a 'double-edged sword', recognised as one of the great iconic narratives but also emphasising members of the military as 'overwhelmingly white, overwhelmingly male, overwhelmingly Anglo-Saxon' (Lieutenant General Morrison in Sales 2015). This was underscored when the serving prime minister of Australia farewelled the Australian and New Zealand troops to Iraq in 2015 by declaring them 'splendid sons of Anzacs' (Greener and Powles 2015). This failed to acknowledge the daughters of Anzacs, as well as those originating from countries other than New Zealand or Australia who also deployed for their country.

This is, moreover, not just an army emphasis. In 2014, the Royal New Zealand Navy conducted a rebranding campaign for their own personnel: 'Warriors of the Sea: Te Taua Moana'. This initiative calls upon the navy's history as the guardian of New Zealand's seas and reminds all that this commitment reflects the 'warrior ethos of the profession of arms we all belong to' (Steer 2014). New Zealand's journalists also reinforce these stereotypes. Karl du Fresne, who regularly covers defence matters, wrote in the *Dominion Post* that it was 'no big surprise that the military is not a happy place for women'. His view was that the military is a centuries-old male institution and that sexual harassment and bullying were inevitable. He does not think any 'sensible woman' would want to join the NZDF (du Fresne 2014). The same author attended a public session on the then upcoming Defence White Paper in 2015 in Wellington, which I also attended in civilian clothing, and commented that in the attendees were 'a surprising number of youngish women' (du Fresne 2015). These public views influence who elects to join the military and, importantly, whether mums, dads, teachers and friends encourage their loved ones to join.

The NZDF needs to achieve a delicate balance between meeting requirements in the modern 'combat culture' so that it can achieve its purpose and ensuring that the negative aspects of this culture do not impede the forces' success. While the warrior culture is essential for mission success when fighting wars, it could potentially be a weakness if it limits diversity and inclusion. Here, then, it is important to note the importance of symbolism. The military is steeped in traditional rituals and artefacts that can reinforce the hegemonic masculinity of the armed forces.

The NZDF could seek to change the artefacts of its culture that are not necessary for combat success but do have an adverse impact on its culture and inclusivity. For instance, military dress is a highly gendered artefact that can serve as a metaphor for the status of women (or men) in an organisation (van Wijk and Finchilescu 2008: 238, 243). In the NZDF the dress is primarily masculine, and in 2014 a new combat uniform was purchased, but no consideration was given to the female body form. It was decided that as women do not represent a large proportion of the organisation then a special fit need not be created. This resulted in some servicewomen feeling that the organisation did not value them and that women did not figuratively or literally 'fit'. Importantly, this has since been rectified, but it demonstrates the symbolic importance of the everyday and apparently mundane factors at play.

On a deeper level, certain rituals also need to be considered in light of the contemporary environment. Traditions may need to adapt and evolve to cater for the new demographic and aspirations for an inclusive military force. There are very important rituals associated with Māori culture, such as the haka, wero (challenge) and pōwhiri (welcome) — but women are excluded from some of those key roles. Again, this potentially presents a paradox of organisational culture in which the formation of a tribe has provided a sense of belonging and identity but has also set up exclusions. One potential enhancement here could be the further development of NZDF kawa (protocol) that allows for fuller participation in all of these important rituals; this is a work in progress. The air force is just now establishing its marae (or more accurately Te Tūrangawaewae o Te Tauaarangi), where authority rests with the air force, though protocols pay due respect to those of the mana whenua, or territorial rights. In May it ran a taiaha training camp to expand and restock its 'diminishing pool of ceremonial warriors' (Wallace 2016: 21). Five women attended this camp. Another alternative route here, instead of pursuing a liberal feminist emphasis on women being able to perform the same roles as men, might be to inculcate a stronger understanding within the NZDF of the valued role of women within Māori society through the notion of sites of equivalence rather than strict duplication of roles. Gender-differentiated roles do not necessarily mean that one gender is valued less than another. Transplanting Pākehā mind-sets into an arena where women and men play different roles, however, has meant that such difference can at times be incorrectly interpreted as one role being lesser than another.

However, it isn't the artefacts themselves that can change a culture; change comes from those who make and remake the underlying values that give those artefacts meaning. Culture keepers, those who keep perpetuating the old values, need to be targeted to deliberately reconstruct the culture (Barsh, Nudelman and Yee 2013). In the NZDF the culture keepers are likely to be in the middle of the organisation: the senior soldiers, the warrant officers and senior non-commissioned officers. That cohort is vital for any kind of cultural change in the NZDF, and there are some signals that changes are under way.

Adapting to the idea of a modern warrior

IN THE MODERN WORLD, PEACE and security missions are extremely complex and full of challenges; there are funding constraints and political pressures associated with their mandates. The goals of gender equality in peacekeeping may, under these conditions, seem an idealistic but not a realistic objective. The path of least resistance, i.e. not including women in untraditional roles, may understandably be considered the best course for mission success. However, as noted, gender equality can improve operational effectiveness and can create a more sustainable peace. The meaningful inclusion of women and, more broadly, gender diversity is, therefore, not just a 'women's issue': it is a leadership and organisational issue. When New Zealand, at the political level, is determining the mission mandate for an operation, it should also consider a gender perspective and make clear requirements for the meaningful inclusion of women. Leaders must not only talk but must also act in ways that ensure that they are champions of change for gender equity (MoD 2014b).

To begin with, New Zealand and the NZDF need to tell more inclusive stories to illustrate the modern warrior — a military icon that has moved on from the Anglo–New Zealand male soldier who displayed acts of courage in battle. The modern military hero should be one who represents the current challenges in contemporary conflicts, such as competition for the support of the population (i.e. human-centric operations). In the idealistic future goal, journalists would tell stories about a doctor who was integral in stopping the spread of a pandemic through her connection with the local population, thus offering a modern reading of the traditional heroic tale. Hollywood would make movies that depicted minorities as military heroes and heroines; *Game of Thrones* and the Hunger Games series have recently displayed some of these ideals.

Admittedly, there have been progressive stories emerging with respect to Anzac with Te Papa's popular exhibition 'Gallipoli: the Scale of Our War', which had at its core five large-scale participants. One was a woman, an army nurse. Peter Ree's book *Anzac Girls* coined a significant name in the title, and its ABC-TVNZ dramatisation was prime-time viewing both in Australia and New Zealand. In 2016, Maria Gill won the Margaret Mahy Book of the Year award with *Anzac Heroes*. In this children's/young adult book (which also won the Elsie Locke non-fiction award), Gill featured several prominent women as Anzac heroines. Indeed, the selection of a woman soldier to adorn the front cover of this very volume is an attempt to take a step in this direction.

The modern warrior is a 'warrior of the psyche', like Professor Michael Evans's stoic philosophy for a soldier: 'an inner citadel of character, rational thought, and moral values' (Evans 2010). A true warrior acts with honour, duty and respect and therefore would embrace the diversity of the contemporary society for the greater good of the NZDF (see Fallows in Jans with Mugford et al. 2013). The Chief of Navy echoed these ideals when he said:

> Being a Warrior is more than putting ourselves into harm's way for our country. It is about standing up for what's right, intervening when we see inappropriate behaviour, speaking up for those who can't speak for themselves. It is about fighting for equality and fairness in everything we do (Press release, Chief of Navy 2014).

Warrior stories, espousing these broader and less-gendered ideals, are the ones that New Zealand and the NZDF need to tell.

And some useful initiatives have begun to pave the way for this goal to be more achievable. The recent Equity Review, the WDSG and an overall growing awareness of gender issues have resulted in specific projects being initiated. March 2016, for example, saw the launch of Operation RESPECT to tackle inappropriate and harmful sexual behaviours in the NZDF. In a media press release, the Chief of Defence Force stated that this operation had been driven by two imperatives: 'looking after the Defence Force's people and recruiting and retaining more military women' (cited in NZDF 2016b). He said that although there had been new approaches to recruiting and retaining women in uniform, new research commissioned by the NZDF showed that being a woman in the NZDF was harder than it should be. Some key action areas noted in that particular press release were: changing the NZDF's culture and behaviours to challenge persistent sexism and better integrate women into the NZDF, and increasing the percentage of women in our armed forces and the representation of women in senior leadership roles. In May 2016, the successful prosecution of a high-profile sexual harassment case involving a naval commander appeared to demonstrate commitment to pursuing these ideals and, perhaps even more importantly, informal indications also suggest some level of change.

There are moves afoot to ensure that this issue is rendered one of importance for *all* personnel. A recent page in the NZDF publication *Force4NZ* (NZDF 2016a), for example, quoted a range of defence force members on why they think we need more military women. Men in particular are seen as drivers of change for issues related to women, given that they are often in positions of power and influence and so can generate political and social will. There are already international men's organisations, such as MenEngage Alliance and the UN Network of Men. New Zealand launched a Champions of Change campaign in November 2015, constituting a group of New Zealand CEOs and chairs who are committed to raising the value of diversity and inclusion within their organisations. Having male champions of change recognises that these are not simply 'women's concerns' but rather global issues that we all have a responsibility to solve. Men have a vital role in achieving transformational change for their mothers, wives, sisters, daughters, colleagues and friends — for the betterment of all.

Conclusion

THE NZDF HAS BEEN A world leader when it comes to gender equity. However, the NZDF currently recognises that little progress has been made in increasing the total percentage of women in the force in recent years, and that, in fact, representation in the last five years has been falling.

The Chief of Defence Force has said that he wants to attract and retain the best individuals for leadership and future capability, recognising that he is missing out on a significant pool of talent. Furthermore, militaries recognise the organisational imperative that, in the face of demographic challenges and rising competition for labour resources, diversity is essential. Diversity is, moreover, an operational effectiveness imperative, with human information domain capability being vital in the modern operating environment (Jans 2014: 4). Therefore, for a range of instrumental reasons the NZDF is taking steps to promote its operational effectiveness by means of an integrated and diverse workforce.

But there are broader motivations for the advancement of the 'gender agenda'. Globally, it is recognised that women, peace and security issues are interlinked, and that mainstreaming a gender perspective can address the underlying gender inequalities and lead to better outcomes for peacemaking initiatives.

Looking ahead, I'd like to see a refreshed, inclusive national identity, reflected in the strategic culture of the NZDF, that truly values diversity. This would be an identity that values and honours our history but has evolved to reflect our modern society. Ideally, my daughter's children and future generations won't consider gender as a barrier to anything. Gender mainstreaming will be a seamlessly integrated part of all aspects of life and there will be no need for women's development groups. Fathers will encourage their daughters to consider the military as a career option, and daughters won't doubt that their mothers are soldiers.

08

Beyond Rote: The New Zealand Army training foreign security forces

Lieutenant Colonel Josh Wineera

> The purpose of training is to tighten up the slack, toughen the body, and polish the spirit. — Morihei Ueshiba

IN THINKING FURTHER ABOUT THE evolution of the New Zealand Army, in early 2015 the Chief of Defence Force (CDF), Lieutenant General Tim Keating, delivered a speech in the Parliamentary Gallery outlining the technical details for a new mission to train Iraqi security forces (Keating 2015a). His speech followed on from Prime Minister John Key's (2015: 1813) announcement that New Zealand would commit troops to support the government of Iraq and the international fight against the Islamic State of Iraq and the Levant (ISIL). Unsurprisingly, the ensuing national debate about such a mission focused on the political nature of the decision and on the failure of previous attempts to build capacity in developing an effective Iraqi security sector.

Few commentators, however, grasped Keating's (2015a: 4) focus on the actual training to be undertaken and the importance of indigenous learning. 'It is not just about how our trainers will teach their counterparts, but it is vital for our trainers to better understand how Iraqi soldiers learn.' This subtle shift in accounting for the learning styles of Iraqi counterparts appears to have been missed by political commentators, media and international relations scholars. Such an approach, though, should have piqued the interest of adult educationalists and those from the training development community.

The attention accorded to indigenous learning here reveals a new addition to the cultural awareness and language training afforded to New Zealand soldiers preparing to instruct their foreign counterparts. As the NZDF has engaged, and will continue to engage, in the practice of building partner capacity and wider security sector reform (SSR), this emphasis on indigenous learning must be synchronised with other SSR practices. Drawing on the literature from adult education, and on SSR in particular, this chapter also draws on military documents, discussions with serving personnel and personal experience. In doing so, it focuses on the New Zealand Army's approach for building partner capacity and training indigenous security forces in contemporary operations in order to better understand the army's attitude towards, and methods of engagement with, other military forces. This chapter serves the purpose of complementing salient points made in earlier chapters.

Reform, capacity building and training

THE PREVAILING LITERATURE ACKNOWLEDGES THE international community's customary approach to assisting the stabilisation of a conflict. The main goals are to transition the conflict into peace, to build a self-sustaining peace and to allow the troubled state to take its place within the 'natural order' of the international system (Coyne 2006: 343; Ottaway 2002: 1001). This is premised on the belief that intervention by third-party countries or external donors is necessary to build (or rebuild) states, which will eventually result in peace. Eizenstat et al. (2005) stress the need to 'foster stable, accountable institutions in struggling nations — institutions that meet the needs of the people, empowering them to improve their lives through lawful, not desperate, means . . . [because] weak and failed countries present a security challenge that cannot be met through security means alone' (135).

The current discourse on training local security forces has, however, seen a change in the terms of how military forces are to best undertake international engagement. The common assertion is that a competent indigenous security sector is not only crucial for enduring stability but also sets the conditions for international donors to exit the recipient country (Bruno 2010; Gates 2010). However, scholars tend to focus on the macro-level structural and institutional theories and concepts of SSR, while policy-makers and practitioners are inclined to establish more narrative explanations of experiences and lessons learned at the micro-level.

Unsurprisingly, in thinking more broadly about the whole concept of 'security sector reform' or the building of capacity, the emphasis on formal institutions of the state is shaped by the conception and experiences of policy-makers and practitioners from the intervening countries or donor organisations. Wesley (2008: 377) contends that recent practices have created the 'regulatory state', and many suggest that there is a propensity to create mirror images of institutions based on the ideal of a Western state (Boas and Jennings 2005). Herein lie a number of rifts in opinion over how this is to be achieved, but the 'template' approach to SSR and capacity building has come under rising pressure, and calls for increased local participation have dominated peace and conflict studies, international security and international relations literature.

Many scholars such as Kaplan (2010), Richmond (2011) and Wesley (2008) thus now vigorously dismiss the notion that a top-down template can be imposed without meaningful regard for local, bottom-up understanding and considerations as part of the state formulation process. In other words, such scholars believe that the Weberian models of a state should not wholly undermine or reject out of hand indigenous practices (Clements et al. 2007). In this vein, the linking of training effectiveness to local practices, or at least an emphasis on understanding indigenous learning styles, would appear to be a highly logical step in

The Afghan National Army Officer Academy in Kabul.

Afghan officer cadets are introduced to the art of camouflage, making use of local flora.

the right direction. As to what capacity building actually *is*, too, there has been a move towards emphasising the role of local stakeholders in deciding policy priorities and in implementing those policies.

For example, the United Nations (UN) is often cited as the prime source for defining capacity building. Within the UN sphere, however, there have been variations over time in defining what constitutes capacity building. The UN Institute for Training and Research thus suggested in 1997 that capacity building is 'generally understood to be the process by which individuals, organisations, institutions and societies build abilities to perform functions, solve problems and achieve objectives' (UNITAR 1997: 1). This statement is silent on the question of who undertakes these actions.

By 2009, however, the United Nations Development Programme (UNDP) defined capacity development as 'the process through which individuals, organizations and societies obtain, strengthen and maintain the capabilities to *set and achieve their own development objectives* over time' (5; emphasis added). Similarly, during the wars in Iraq and Afghanistan the US military implemented major programmes that were intended to create 'an environment that fosters host-nation institutional development, community participation, human resources development and strengthening managerial systems' (US Army 2008: 1–8). So the theoretical and policy literature has increasingly come to view engagement and encouragement of local ideas, priorities and processes as being key to increasing the likelihood of successful capacity building and, therefore, to the aims of SSR.

In addition to this emphasis on local engagement, there is also an emphasis on SSR as constituting something that contributes to a country's development as well as to its security. Thus the training, coaching or mentoring of individuals and groups of security forces is increasingly included within the UNDP remit (UNDP 2009), as well as within the UN Department of Peacekeeping Operations and, as expected, in others' military operations (US Joint Chiefs of Staff 2010: V-4). This is because the objective of this technical assistance is to help partner governments to provide effective, legitimate and accountable security for their citizens, which will also help foster economic development, political stability and social cohesion. This moves beyond the mere provision of equipment and training, given that security personnel can better carry out their responsibilities if the institutional and governance frameworks necessary to sustain them are equally well-developed. However, the call to train local security forces tends to pursue an old framework of capacity-building programmes. Donor governments (and other organisations) are still typically committed to fairly one-dimensional 'train and equip' programmes. Critics have argued that this form of engagement represents regression back to the type of assistance symbolic of the cold war (Channa 2002; Panarelli 2010), and more attention is now being paid to how military forces engage in these practices.

In terms of building military partner capacity and SSR, then, academics and practitioners have tended to focus on *what* should be taught. Few, however, have critically examined *how* the training is taught. The NZDF efforts in Iraq and Afghanistan provide opportunities to consider this question of 'how' New Zealand military personnel seek to undertake the training of other military forces. Before we begin this investigation, however, a consideration of military training in general will help set the scene.

Rote learning

TO UNDERSTAND HOW LOCAL SECURITY forces might be trained, it is important to comprehend how the intervening (international) security force learns and trains itself. This can be termed as the institution's learning identity. Security forces, particularly Western military forces, emphasise duty, tradition, obedience and rote learning (Scott 1971).

According to Murray, 'rote learning is a valuable tool for [military] training' (2014: 11). Carter (2010: 170) further asserts that 'repetition, drill and rote memorization are the hallmark of military training'. Learning by rote is thus said to be a prescriptive military approach, with the product of almost robotic action. Conformity and uniformity are the aim. Prominent psychologist Walter Pillsbury stressed that the 'skill increases with each repetition as is shown by the quickness with which the movement will be performed and the adequacy of each movement' (1938: 2). The speed of repetition in rote memory increases with practice, and in practical physical application it can eliminate unnecessary actions, thereby creating greater efficacy.

At the individual level, that of a soldier, rote learning remains the easiest method of learning. Breaking down tasks into more manageable, smaller, and linear steps is the common technique. Soldiers are inculcated and instructed to carry out all manner of drills and routines (see Harding, this volume). These are designed to bring a degree of predictability about how individuals will act and react. The expected response gives the surety needed to meld and synchronise team actions. This is particularly evident in mass mobilisation, when a citizen army is raised to fight, as was the case in the first and second world wars. While many educationalists decry such a mechanistic approach to learning, military necessity is often cited as the rationale for adopting a system that provides the bare essentials to quickly assemble a fighting capacity. Predictably, intervening forces charged with building the capacity of local security forces have, in the main, adopted this same approach.

The theory of 'instructional design' as an educational theory about teaching military personnel was pioneered by Robert Gagné (1974). Gagné's relationship with the military began with his work in the US Army Air Corps in the Second World War. Essentially, his theory stipulates that there are several different types or levels of learning. The significance of these classifications is that each different type requires different types of instruction. Gagné identified five major categories of learning: verbal information, intellectual skills, cognitive strategies, motor skills, and attitudes. He also further developed nine key instructional events (see Table 1) to help sort how an instructor and learner might engage.

Table 1. Robert Gagné's nine key instructional events. Adapted from Gagné and Medsker 1996: 140.

INSTRUCTOR/DESIGNER	ACTION RESPONSE OF LEARNER
1. Gaining learner's attention	Readiness
2. Stating session objectives	Knowing what to expect
3. Reminding what was done before	Stimulation of long-term memory
4. Highlighting key features	Perceiving what is important
5. Structuring learning	Creating links and associations
6. Encouraging activity	Performing
7. Providing feedback	Learning awareness and satisfaction
8. Evaluating progress	Strengthening learning
9. Signalling future learning	Gaining learning overview

Gagné insisted that 'trainers need to guide learners when the learning goals [are] specific and well structured, as is typically the case in military training' (Spector 2000: 219). This approach is a repeatable, step-by-step process for developing training materials and evaluating the effectiveness of an instructional event (Swain 2005). It was intended to create an experience that made the acquisition of knowledge and skill more efficient, effective and appealing (Morrison et al. 2010; Jonassen 2001; Reigeluth 1999). The goal is communication or transfer of knowledge to learners (Bednar et al. 1995), and in most cases the example used is to break down a task into small steps.

The repeatable, repetitive components of some of Gagné's instructional theory reinforce a rote style of learning. However, while they have

Iraqi soldiers parade at the end of their formal training in Taji Camp.

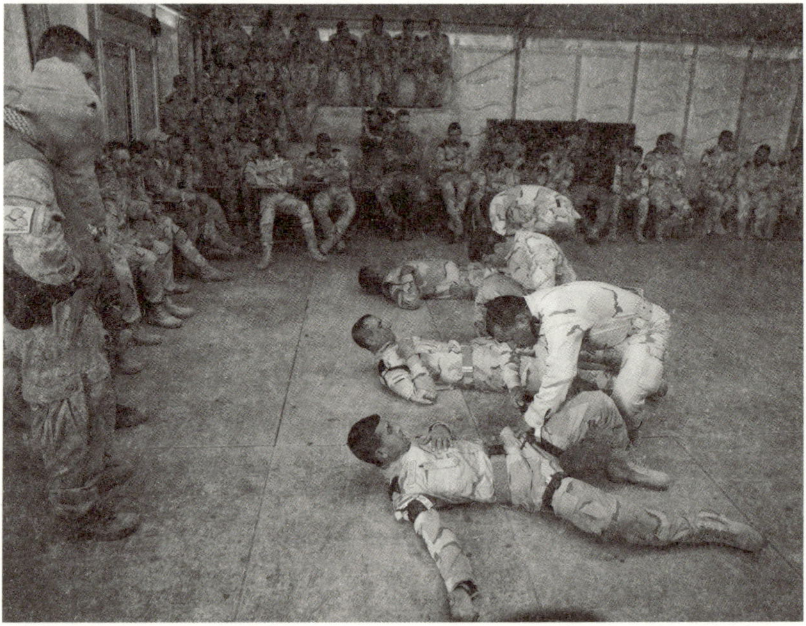

New Zealand Army trainers watch over Iraqi soldiers during medical training.

proved convenient for quickly producing capacity in military mass, the contemporary operating environment is one that has forced new thinking of training and, especially, instructional design. Swain (2005) observes that 'senior [US] Army Leaders responsible for training are asking whether a thirty-year-old instructional system design process can be effective for today's Army' (2). This reflects the learning and knowledge gap in preparing for combat against predictable and symmetrical armies as opposed to adversaries that behave in an asymmetrical manner. This is more commonly known as preparing for the wrong opponent.

Beyond rote learning

THE MODERN-DAY SECURITY ENVIRONMENT HAS compelled Western military services to re-evaluate their 'robotic' training. 'Shooting automatons' are not what is required (Liebknecht 1973: 24). Instead, modern militaries need a soldier who, rather than merely learning by rote, also learns actively and knows how to think and to 'learn meaningfully' (Novak 1998: 65). Sullivan (2010) sums up these ideas when he asserts:

> Rote learning is no longer sufficient to produce the kind of problem-solving soldiers the Army needs for today's complicated challenges. Adaptability, critical thinking and creativity have become critical skills for modern soldiers, and the Army is changing the way it trains and educates to ensure that those skills are instilled in its warriors (v).

Education scholar Malcolm Knowles is one of the principal influencers of military adult learning and instructional design in responding to these challenges. Knowles, a strong advocate of self-directed learning and the teacher's role as a facilitator[1] in the process of adult education,

---

1. In the military this role is more commonly referred to as an instructor.

is well-recognised for his theory of andragogy.

Andragogy is, according to Knowles, a theory that is 'vastly in contrast with the traditional pedagogical model and it advocates both the self-directed learning concept and the teacher as the facilitator of learning' (1990: 57). Knowles (1980) and many other scholars have long argued that adults must be taught differently from children, given that their learning process differs drastically from the traditional pedagogical approach (see also Brookfield 1986; Caffarella 1993; Collins 1991; and Cotton 1995). Importantly, too, the adult education literature suggests that adults are motivated to devote energy to learn something to the extent that they perceive it will help them perform tasks or deal with problems they confront in their life situations. Furthermore, they learn new knowledge, understandings, skills, values and attitudes most effectively when these are aligned to real-life situations (Birzer 2003).

Andragogy thus presents a sea change away from the traditional rote form of learning and training delivery. This has dictated a change in military curriculums. Military academies now find it advantageous to deviate from the mechanical and behavioural aspects of training and to evolve into training programmes that inform security forces how to identify, respond to and solve problems. It is essential that training be conducted in such a way as to be as meaningful as possible, and training for a contemporary operating environment is 'a lesson in understanding self as well as others' (Spencer 2010: 27).

Thus, in applying these ideas to the training of soldiers, it is now deemed essential that soldiers learn how to think critically, conceptually and even creatively, when confronted with vague and changing situations. They must also have the ability to adapt learning from their own experiences. Moreover, the need to know the reason for learning and becoming skilled in a subject that has immediate relevance is apparent. Spencer (2010), referring to the ability to perform in the modern conflict environment, stresses that 'more than just equipping and training soldiers . . . it requires those who thrive in ambiguity, complexity and change' (27). For those in leadership positions, there comes the obligation to get subordinates to think and act differently from previous inflexible actions (Kolenda 2012).

The earlier work of Gagné and the more recent work of Knowles offer important theoretical insights into how Western security forces themselves typically learn and train. It is with this understanding that the transference of knowledge from international security trainers to local security forces in an SSR capacity-building context can be further examined, but first we consider the rise in importance of such efforts.

When training locals becomes critical

IF THE STANDARD STARTING POINT for launching an SSR programme is a dysfunctional security sector, i.e. one that does not provide effective security for the state and its people, then for the last several years Iraq and Afghanistan have most certainly been cases in point. For the US military, developing the capability and capacity of foreign indigenous security forces and their institutions in Iraq and Afghanistan was, and is, a critical mission. Indeed, Secretary of Defense Robert Gates (2007) even asserted that 'arguably the most important military component in the War on Terror[ism] is not the fighting we do ourselves, but how well we enable and empower our partners to defend and govern themselves'.

In Iraq as late as 2005, however, there had appeared to be no immediate urgency to create a reform programme to build a professional, non-political military representative of the country (Sedra 2010). Yet the realisation soon came to the US government that a vital component of its exit strategy would be conditional on the Iraqi security forces' ability to take over responsibility for their country's security. Fellows (2005) chronicled this sentiment by President Bush and senior officials, who regularly insisted that '[a]s Iraqis stand up we will stand down'. What followed was a massive increase in the US effort to train more Iraqi soldiers and police (Cordesman and Mausner 2007; Malkasian 2007; Robinson 2008).

In the case of SSR in Afghanistan, Murray (2011) criticised police reform efforts, pointing out that while the training was 'largely delivered by operational police', the achievement of certain objectives was sabotaged by 'ineffective training methods, poor learning material, bad examples and sometimes out of date information' (119). Most importantly for the purposes of this chapter, Murray argued that 'the inexperienced trainers make little use of proven adult learning techniques, such as group discussions, scenarios, role playing and analysis of case histories, which promote participation, learning and retention of information' (ibid.). Evidently, the application of rote learning for the Afghan National Police was insufficient, and poor instructional constructs further compounded the problems.

A natural question that arises from these examples, and from the continuing problems plaguing SSR efforts worldwide, is this: Are there cases where local security forces have been meaningfully considered as part of the capacity-building effort? Has the contextualisation of transferring knowledge been formed at the local level, in which the international security force has adapted to local forces, rather than the other way around? Another more specific question then arises: How has New Zealand pursued its partner training and capacity-building programmes?

The New Zealand Army's approach

THE NEW ZEALAND ARMY PROVIDES the mainstay of personnel for the building partner capacity training missions in Iraq and Afghanistan. Both missions are characterised by an emphasis on partnership — that is, with the Iraqi Security Forces (ISF) and Afghan National Army (ANA).

For the present time, operational security restrictions are in place in

Evaluating Iraqi soldiers during one of the final phases of their training.

Physical training — carrying a wounded comrade to safety.

Iraq, with even the names of army trainers (both previous and current) remaining classified (see Baguioro 2016: 9). However, aspects of their preparations in New Zealand and engagement with the indigenous forces in theatre can be discussed, and they highlight the nuanced and deliberate shift in accounting for the learning styles of their counterparts. CDF Keating (2015a) foreshadowed the intent of the NZDF's attitude towards the mission in Iraq when he said: 'What is apparent is that the Iraqis must be fully integrated into the development and the delivery of training. *True partnership means working together*' (4; emphasis added).

For the mission in Iraq, a comprehensive pre-deployment training strategy for the first contingent of trainers was designed by a team of experts and specialists in a variety of fields. This team included linguists, training evaluators, coaches and mentors, and irregular warfare specialists. The design team also looked deeply into cross-cultural adult training and cross-cultural adult learning (NZDF 2015a). The inclusion of experts specialising in adult training and adult learning across cultures signalled an effort to stretch beyond previous curriculums that had simply been based on the typical content of 'general culture and language'.

A feature of the curriculum for the first pre-deployment sessions focused on understanding the New Zealand military (Western) style of delivering instruction, and of teaching and training (see P. Greener, this volume, for a critique of the NZDF on this point in previous deployments). Understanding one's teaching identity reminded the trainers that their normalised view and approach in the classroom were principally based on learning symmetry within a New Zealand context. That is, the notion that there would be a high degree of consonance and correspondence between themselves as trainers and their usual New Zealand military training audience. The Gagné-like instructional idiosyncrasies then further alerted the trainers that, while they might be well-intentioned and competent, they may not appreciate or understand the effect their

Morning Lessons Wednesday, 11 March 2015

MODULE 1: TRAINING FOREIGN SECURITY FORCES AND EVALUATING SUCCESS		
0800–0830	Training foreign security forces: Iraq then, Iraq now	An outline of CTC training 15. A summary of the past and present efforts to train the ISF and an overview of the NZ Govt and NZDF strategic and operational context for OP MANAWA.
0840–0920	How your ISF counterpart/ trainee learns and best responds to a foreign trainer	A review of practices and techniques that help connect and build rapport with ISF counterpart/trainee. Lessons and methods to appreciate the indigenous cultural and learning aspects of the ISF.
0920–1000	The NZDF trainer: How we instruct, and recognising our biases and idiosyncrasies	A summary of NZDF instructional practices and techniques and modifications to better connect with the counterpart/trainee. This session poses various situations for discussion and consideration in small groups.
1000–1040	Morning tea and informal Q&A with Module 1 instructors	
1040–1120	Starting with the end in mind: The value of evaluating, and your part in the Master Training and Evaluation Programme (MTEP)	A review of evaluation practices and techniques and the relationship to measuring effectiveness and measuring success of a building partner capacity mission. The session will also explain a recommended method and process to capture validation and evaluation data for short loop and high-level analysis.
1120–1200	What is training, coaching, advising and mentoring (TCAM)? When should they be applied?	This period will define training, coaching, advising and mentoring (TCAM) according to best practices and past lessons. The difference between mechanistic, rote-type skills instruction and the soft-skill approach needed to better advise and mentor will be explained.
1200–1300	Lunch and all instructors available for informal Q&A	

Selected extract of NZDF pre-deployment curriculum for OP MANAWA. (OP MANAWA is the NZDF code name assigned to the building partner capacity training mission in Taji Camp, Iraq.) NEW ZEALAND ARMY COLLECTIVE TRAINING CENTRE.

teaching style would have on their Iraqi students.

A further component of the curriculum explained to the trainers the general learning levels, learning habits and the more common learning styles that their Iraqi students might exhibit and best respond to. In preparing for this, the pre-deployment design team examined numerous reports from the Republic of Iraq Ministry of Education, as well as analysing adult and youth literacy data from international sources, such as the United Nations (UNESCO 2012; UNDP 2014).

While combat planners might have been bemused at the emphasis on investigating educational statistics and revising Western instructional practices, educational and training development professionals would quickly acknowledge the necessity for undertaking a training needs and literacy needs analysis prior to engaging in that training (Clarke 2003; Reardon 2010; Salas and Cannon-Bowers 2001).

As to the success of this new form of training package, the most recent government review of the training mission to Iraq (NZDF 2015b) appeared to affirm that it is performing well and achieving the agreed objectives. 'The training is having a tangible and positive impact,' cited the review (1). Political commentator Tracey Watkins remarked: 'It only took a day watching the Kiwi trainers and their students in action at Camp Taji to know they are offering real support and it is more than just a drop in the ocean' (4). The training measures themselves remain classified, however, which leaves open the question as to whether the outcome is causally linked or correlated to the preparation training.

Prior to 2014 the NZDF contributed two principal missions in Afghanistan. These were Special Forces and a Provincial Reconstruction Team (PRT).

In 2013 the New Zealand government announced a new mission, focused on training Afghan officer cadets (Coleman and McCully 2013). This would be to support a British-led initiative to establish the Afghan National Army Officer Academy (ANAOA). Drawing on the UK's Royal

Military Academy Sandhurst (RMAS) officer training model,[2] ANAOA would 'harness the best characteristics of RMAS, tailored to suit the Afghan context and Afghan National Army (ANA), in order to deliver high standard training for junior officers' (RMAS 2014: 5).

The New Zealand Army's contribution has been and remains modest in terms of numbers compared with the previous decade in Afghanistan. OP RUA II consists of eight personnel supplementing the UK training at ANAOA.[3] In early 2014 the author was requested to deliver a small preparation curriculum to the second contingent prior to their departure. Subsequently the author was invited to deliver a similar curriculum to the third and fourth contingents. As with the 2015 Iraq pre-deployment programme, the trainers were introduced to some of the learning tendencies and learning styles that the cadets and their Afghan counterparts might display and best respond to. Emphasis was placed on the need to demonstrate to the Afghans that the New Zealand trainers were sincere in their learning empathy with the indigenous habits. An example was the trainers trying to understand that for many of the cadets their learning influence might have come from group problem solving, rather than as an individual. Thus, the trainers were gradually introduced to the educational approach known as cooperative learning, or what Johnson and Johnson (2002) term 'learning together and alone'. The experience of observing and delivering the curriculum was presented to the National Centre for Peace and Conflict Studies (Wineera 2014) (see overleaf).

Typically the New Zealand Army style of teaching is focused on individualistic learning, with competition between learners encouraged. Consequentially, by reflecting on the normative New Zealand teaching

---

2. Sandhurst is recognised as one of the world's most prestigious officer cadet training institutes.
3. OP RUA I was the code name for the small, two-person army training teams assigned to British forces from late 2000. See Urlich 2011. OP RUA II is the NZDF code name assigned to the building partner capacity training mission for ANAOA. This contingent normally consists of eight New Zealand Army personnel.

Training us to train them

Observations of NZ military advisors preparing to train Afghan army officer cadets

Josh Wineera, PhD Student
National Centre for Peace and Conflict Studies

Background

In 2013 the New Zealand Provincial Reconstruction Team (PRT) was withdrawn from Afghanistan. The New Zealand Government decided to continue supporting peacebuilding efforts and agreed to deploy a small contingent of soldiers in a training role. Late last year the first team of trainers joined their British, Australian, Norwegian, and Danish counterparts at the Afghan National Army Officer Academy in Kabul.

In March 2014 I was invited to observe and support the preparation of the second contingent of trainers before they deployed to Afghanistan. I was provided with the preparation syllabus and offered the chance to speak with the trainers for 2 two-hour sessions. I prepared two talks based on a cross-section of historical and contemporary literature. I also developed a rudimentary back-casting scenario using key events that have occurred in Afghanistan in the past 20-years to illustrate the impact on education and learning of a fictitious Afghan cadet.

This opportunity allowed me to connect with my field of enquiry, establish personal contacts and re-confirm the gap in the research.

Syllabus analysed, practices observed

- ✧ Basic language and cultural awareness sessions incorporated in to the programme
- ✧ No formal training or exposure to cross-cultural teaching, indigenous learning theories or learning styles
- ✧ No sense of education history and learning influences of the average cadet likely to enter the academy
- ✧ No sense of the big picture, security sector reform, capacity building, linkages between the security institutions and the 'fielded force', oversight and governance, connecting the macro and micro changes
- ✧ Experiential learning by the trainers themselves most likely on arrival in Kabul. Most information sharing and 'lessons-learned' will be exchanged during the hand-over with the trainers they replace

- ✧ *Assume, good trainers can naturally adapt*
- ✧ *Assume, only technical assistance needed*
- ✧ *Assume, NZ soldiers will naturally build rapport and gain respect*

The education and learning of cadet 'Arman'

A back-casting scenario

Linkages and benefits to my research

- ✧ Security Sector Reform, preparation of trainers from donor countries/organisations
- ✧ 'It's not just about how we teach but also about how they learn'
- ✧ Is this a re-run of Cold-War military aid or a new form of more personal interface in international relations?
- ✧ Many studies of Security Sector Reform at the structural macro top-level. Fewer studies at the micro bottom-level, particularly related to curricula and syllabi for donor trainer preparation
- ✧ Curious about indigenous learning theory and utility for trainers
- ✧ Thinking about theoretical framework and methodology, possible comparative research method of syllabi from case study organisations that prepare trainers, coaches, advisors and mentors
- ✧ Thinking about experimental research design with indigenous learning theory as the intervening variable in to syllabi where it is not currently present. Ethics approval, probabilistic sampling methods

Theory: Indigenous learning knowledge is positively related to trainer capabilities.

Selection of References

- ✧ Blac, J. S., & Mendenhall, M. (1990). Cross-Cultural Training Effectiveness: A review and a theoretical framework for future research. *Academy of Management Review, 15* (1), 113-136.
- ✧ Coffe, H., & Geys, B. (2007). Towards an Empirical Characterization of Bridging and Bonding Social Capital. *Nonprofit and Voluntary Sector Quarterly* 36.1, 121-139.
- ✧ Dicum, D. (2008). Learning War, and Emergencies: A Study of of the Learners Perspective. *Comparative Education Review, 52* (4), 619-638.
- ✧ Gerspacher, N. (2012). *Preparing Advisers for Capacity-Building Missions.* US Institute for Peace.
- ✧ Ramsey, R. D. (2006). *Advice for Advisors: Suggestions and Observations from Lawrence to the Present.* Government Printing Office.
- ✧ Rosen, F. F. (2011). No Words will Deliver Anything: coaching and mentoring as neoliberal governance strategy in the Afghan state administration. *Journal of Intervention and Statebuilding* 5.2: 151-173.
- ✧ Samady, S. R. (2001). *Education and Afghan Society in the twentieth century.* Paris, France: UNESCO.
- ✧ UNESCO. (2012). *UNESCO Country Programming Document (UCPD) Afghanistan 2013-2015.* Kabul, Afghanistan: UNESCO.
- ✧ Zbylut, M, (2008). *An analysis of cross-cultural behavior for military advisors in the Middle-East.* Army Research Institute for the Behavioral and Social Sciences, Alexandria, VA.

Poster presented to the National Centre for Peace and Conflict Studies, University of Otago.

practices, the trainers could contextualise their part in the upskilling of the Afghan cadets and their Afghan instructor counterparts and adapt their delivery to optimise the transference of military knowledge. Rote, mechanistic learning still pervades, but the idea would be to quickly get beyond rote training in order to move into the more interpersonal, mentoring 'soft space' where conversations could take place to discuss the values and ethics of being a soldier. Training a person to shoot a rifle is relatively easy; talking with them as to when it's not right to shoot someone is the hard part. The key therefore is to quickly establish learning rapport as a mentor, where the demonstration of empathy by the New Zealander is genuine, as shown by the willingness to understand the way that the cadet or counterparts learn.

Outside of the military, training professionals are often unnerved at the thought of training foreign security forces. At the New Zealand Association for Training Development (NZATD) annual conference (2014) a public presentation on coaching and mentoring for OP RUA II elicited a number of comments from the assembled training professionals. On seeing an image of indigenous soldiers being taught weapon drills, Keri Scrimshaw (2014) tweeted '. . . one of the more daunting training audiences I've seen'.

Unlike the training mission to Iraq, the names of the New Zealand Army trainers in Afghanistan are not classified. Trainer and mentor Major Roger Earp has been one of the most prominent army officers to document and speak about his team's OP RUA II mission. Earp is a regular speaker at army contemporary warfare conferences, and his was one of the first contingents to be introduced to indigenous learning styles during the New Zealand phase of the pre-deployment curriculum. His subsequent analysis and documentation of his mentoring experience (2016) reveals an approach that sought to adapt to the local methods, rather than the other way round, stressing that 'we would do things their way, not our way, whenever possible — a concept we later coined "Afghanising"' (3).

The value of New Zealanders at ANAOA has been recognised by Afghan

Defence Minister Abdullah Habibi, who has acknowledged the NZDF's contribution. At a recent graduation of 320 officer cadets, Lieutenant Colonel Andrew Brown and Staff Sergeant Brian King were awarded Chief Mentor Commendations for their work (NZDF 2016d).

Conclusion

THE NEW ZEALAND ARMY HAS continued to adapt its training practices from outdated and outmoded training programmes. The incorporation of local indigenous learning techniques for pre-deployment is, in particular, a significant and useful change — as is broader institutional recognition of the army's teaching identity and a growing awareness of the concomitant need for adaptation to local practices. Indeed, the real strength of the New Zealand Army more generally lies in this adaptability and responsiveness. The army's ability to assemble from within its existing ranks a whole cadre of soldiers that can readily deploy, and which recognises the nuances of training a foreign force, is key to this strength. What these soldiers are increasingly cognisant of is that it is not just about how 'we' teach but also how 'they' learn.

That there is emphasis on appreciating the impact of educational scholars such as Knowles and Gagné within the New Zealand Army reveals a more sophisticated and comprehensive approach to building partner capacity in a security sector reform context that might otherwise be assumed. Understanding adult learning theory better, as well as comprehending the methods of instruction that would require change within the group being trained, has gained importance within the organisation.

Furthermore, this move to go beyond approaches based on simple rote learning holds broader promise. For example, if one of the key goals of a trainer is to build rapport, then exhibiting learning empathy as well as cultural empathy provides for a formalised space that can extend training into more interpersonal and positive behavioural actions. This means that understanding learning styles may not just be useful in and of itself for training, but may also be more far-reaching in terms of utility across other missions.

The New Zealand Army, and indeed the New Zealand Defence Force as a whole, has 'a long and proud tradition of training and partnering other security forces' (Keating 2015a: 1). While pride and tradition do have a place in anchoring training efforts, smart adaptations and ongoing improvement to better understand the partner-learner are essential. And the training results that continue to flow back from the missions in Iraq and Afghanistan look promising.

09

The Limits of the Military Instrument

W. J. Fish, B. K. Greener, N. Harding and C. Sigley

CARL VON CLAUSEWITZ FAMOUSLY ARGUED that military force was an extension of politics. As a corollary of this, he also warned of the need for military officers to recognise the limitations of the military and to ensure that their political masters were clear as to where military limits lay. In his *Two Letters on Strategy* he thus asserted that the main obligation of military leaders was to 'prevent policy from making demands *that are contrary to the nature of war*, to save it from misusing the military instrument from a failure to understand what it can and cannot do' (1984: 25; italics in original). Von Clausewitz's advice about not making undue or inappropriate demands of the military instrument need not apply only to war, but rather to all instances in which that military instrument might conceivably be called upon to act in contemporary times.

The proliferation and range of missions that military personnel are nowadays asked to engage in — peace support operations, stability operations, operations other than war, humanitarian assistance and disaster relief (HADR) operations — has seen those personnel drawn into a number of roles other than traditional war-fighting. Recognising this suggests that we need to attend to von Clausewitz's warning about understanding what the military instrument 'can and cannot do'. What are the limitations of the military, and is this communicated to political leaders?

In this chapter, we focus on the first part of this question: Of the roles that the military might conceivably be tasked with, what can and can't they actually do?

Here we begin with a consideration of what it means to 'be able to' do something. We then move to ask why military personnel may believe that they 'can' undertake policing tasks before considering why police personnel might think that they (military personnel) 'cannot' do these tasks. We then consider models of civil–military relations and possible future options to suggest how practitioners might best be aware of, respond to and diminish risks associated with the limits of the military instrument in contemporary operations.

In this chapter Fish initially utilises a philosophical type of method and approach — that is, rather than emphasise narrative in these opening stages he analyses the core notion of 'being able to' in the style of philosophical modes of enquiry. The chapter then draws on a previous qualitative social science project wherein Fish and Greener conducted more than 60 interviews with serving military and police personnel about their views on military and police roles in peace and stability operations. We then utilise the ethnographic anthropological work undertaken by Harding, already noted in this volume, in understanding why military personnel might be disposed to think they 'can' undertake certain tasks.

The personal and professional policing expertise of Sigley is then called upon to help discuss and identify the kinds of concerns that police officers have with this claim. These force-specific perspectives are then brought together to identify where some of the limits of the military instrument lie. The chapter then addresses the question of the appropriateness of military forces resisting political pressure to engage in tasks that lie outside their limits, by exploring military sociological models for civil–military relations. We close by considering possible best practices in developing how the military might work best with other agencies in responding to a range of security and other issues into the future.

Having an ability

IN ASKING WHAT MILITARY FORCES 'can' do, we must first explore what it is for an agent to have an ability to perform some action or task. Philosophical discussions of how to evaluate claims that an agent 'can' do something can be found as far back as Aristotle (who, in the *Metaphysics*, rejects the claim that an agent can *only* do what they are *actually* doing). In more recent discussions of these issues, Honoré (1964), borrowing an example from British philosopher and legal theorist John Austin, asks us to consider a competent golfer who must hole a short putt to win a game (463). Honoré points out that we might reasonably ask, of the golfer, 'Can she hole this putt?' (Imagine a commentator uttering that sentence in hushed tones.) In this sense, we are wondering whether the golfer will succeed on this very occasion. For this reason, Honoré calls this the *particular* sense of 'can'.

Honoré argues that, in the particular sense, the answer to whether or not she *can* hole the putt is given by whether or not she *does* hole the putt: 'If the golfer tried [her] best to sink the putt and failed, then, in the particular sense of 'can', [she] could not sink it' (464). If this is correct, then in this particular sense, the claim that 'I can do such-and-such' seems to be equivalent to the claim that 'nothing prevents me from doing such-and-such'. If something prevents the golfer from making the putt, he suggests — be it nerves, a rogue gust of wind or an unseen bump on the green — then this makes it the case that she *could not* make the putt (on this occasion). Although other objections have been raised to this analysis, for present purposes the most significant problem with an analysis of 'can' in terms of 'nothing prevents me' is that it is implausible for what Honoré calls the *general* use of 'can'. In the case of the competent golfer, the *general* sense of 'can' can be seen when we consider that the very fact that the golfer is competent means that it must be true that she *can* hole a short putt, even if as it happens she fails on this occasion (465).

To approach the distinction between general and particular abilities from a different direction, imagine the following interchange: I ask you if you can swim, you say you can, I ask you to show me. Unless we are at a swimming pool (or other appropriate place), you would not be able to swim there and then. So — right then and there — you cannot swim. Yet this doesn't impugn your original claim: when you answered my question in the affirmative, you were asserting that you had a general ability to swim (which you could exercise in appropriate circumstances), not that you had the particular ability to swim right then and there. To have the general ability to swim, then, is to have the ability to swim when in circumstances in which swimming is possible.

If it is true, in the general sense, that you can swim, then this cannot mean that nothing ever prevents you from swimming! As we have just seen, you can be able to swim (in the general sense), yet be unable to swim (in the particular sense) if you happen to be away from a suitable body of water. And the same is true for the competent golfer. It is true, in the general sense, that a competent golfer can hole a short putt; this doesn't mean that nothing ever prevents such a golfer from sinking a short putt — even the most skilful golfers sometimes miss. To interpret the general sense of 'can' as equivalent to 'nothing prevents me', then, we would have to read 'nothing prevents me' as something like 'it is not impossible for me'. And while it is evident that if a competent golfer *can* hole a short putt it is not impossible for that golfer to hole a short putt, these statements are nonetheless not equivalent as the converse does not hold: while it is not *impossible* for a non-golfer such as myself to hole a short putt — if you give me enough balls and enough time I'll eventually get one in — this does not show that I *can* hole a short putt in the general sense. Or, to make the point another way, it is clearly not impossible for me to draw the ace of spades from a regular deck of cards with my eyes closed — I might get lucky, after all — but this does not go any way to showing that I have a reliable general ability to draw an ace of spades from a regular deck with my eyes closed.

So while we might think there is a case for interpreting 'can' as 'nothing prevents me' in the particular case, it will not work for the general case. So when we say that a competent golfer 'can' hole a short putt in the general sense — or that a competent golfer has the general ability to hole a short putt — what are we saying? Well, as we have seen, we are not saying that a competent golfer will make every single putt they attempt, nor are we saying that the fact that I will eventually make a putt suffices to make me a competent golfer. According to Honoré, then, when we use 'can' in this general sense:

> What we usually mean by saying that a person can do an action of a certain type is not that he may do it . . . but rather that he normally succeeds when he tries (465; see also Nowell-Smith 1960: 96).

This interpretation explains our intuitions about both the competent golfer — even though they do occasionally miss, they normally succeed (when they try) — and me: even though I occasionally hole the putt (when I get lucky), I do not normally succeed. Likewise in the case of swimming: your ability to swim means that, when the circumstances allow for swimming, you can move through the water successfully; my inability to swim means that I will not reliably succeed at this, even in appropriate circumstances.

These ideas come together in the following way. To have the general ability to perform an action, your succeeding at that task need not be infallible — we can all make mistakes — but it should be suitably robust or reliable. As Kaufman has it, 'in the case of an ability like shooting accurately, it seems plausible to suppose that *a consistent record of success* is ample evidence of the presence of an ability, even on those infrequent occasions of failure' (1963: 538, our emphasis). If you have such a general ability to swim, then, to have a particular ability to swim — to be able to swim right here and now — is for there to be nothing that prevents you from exercising that general ability: that is, nothing that prevents you from swimming. Likewise, to have a particular ability to hole the short putt you are currently addressing is to have the general ability to hole short putts *plus* for there to be nothing that prevents you from making the putt on this particular occasion.

When we look at the ability to perform police tasks, then, we can assume that civilian police forces (such as New Zealand Police) have the general ability to perform police tasks. (After all, if they did not, it would be difficult to explain why we still keep them around — see Greener and Fish 2011 for further discussion). The problem is that, as things currently stand, they lack the particular ability to perform police tasks in post-conflict environments. This is because a range of aspects of post-conflict environments function to prevent civilian police from exercising this general ability. Not only is it the case that civilian police have no built-in expeditionary capability and are typically reliant on others for transport, logistics and accommodation when in mission (Goldsmith and Harris 2010), but also civilian police already have a domestic role to play, and it can be politically difficult to remove them from this role. Most significantly, however, the hostility of post-conflict environments renders it unacceptably dangerous to deploy civilian police: just as a swimmer needs a swimming pool in order to have the particular ability to swim, a civilian police officer needs a relatively benign environment in order to have the particular ability to police.

This is why it can look appealing to use military forces in this space: the force protection capabilities of military forces means that they are not prevented from operating in impermissible environments in the way that police forces are. So the things that prevent police forces from exercising their general ability need not prevent military forces. The military may thus appear 'able' to police in environments where traditional police forces are 'unable' to do so. Yet although this absence of prevention might support the assumption that military forces have the particular ability to police post-conflict environments ('might', because it would require that nothing else happened to prevent them from succeeding on a given occasion), it would only do so if it has already been established that military forces have the *general* ability to perform police tasks. So our question becomes: Do military forces have, or can they acquire, such a general ability?

Having the ability to police

IT MUST BE STRESSED THAT in interviews conducted for Greener and Fish (2015), New Zealand Army interviewees had a number of concerns about being tasked with policing roles. They were aware that they had their own roles to play; concerns about military operational effectiveness should they also have to undertake policing roles abounded. As a number of the interviewees wondered, 'How are we supposed to do our jobs well if we are doing someone else's job too?' Increased risk was also emphasised — not only the risk of negatively affecting the immediate military objectives at hand, but also the risks inherent in modelling military engagement in internal security in countries where stability was scarce and democratic politics fledgling. Most suggested, therefore, that they 'shouldn't' (particularly that they 'shouldn't be seen to be doing policing in a green uniform') and certainly didn't 'want' to undertake policing tasks in situations such as those mentioned above. However, some, albeit reluctantly, at times said that if absolutely necessary, they 'could' perform policing tasks.

There are a number of reasons why military forces might have this attitude. For one thing, since the 1990s the range of demands placed upon military personnel has widened significantly. Traditional cold-war peacekeeping placed fairly limited demands upon military (and civilian) personnel, as the key roles involved were typically those of patrolling, monitoring and reporting on ceasefires. The so-called 'second generation' peacekeeping operations that emerged in the 1990s, however, saw military personnel being drawn into new roles. In overseas peace or stability-type operations, such as in Panama, for example, 'the US military, as the only entity in the country with the capacity to provide the level of stability required, had to deal with the lack of a viable and functioning security apparatus' (Jayamaha et al. 2010: 21), and they therefore attempted to undertake internal security roles themselves. More generally, recent developments in British (UK MoD 2009: 223) and US (US Army Marine Corps 2007: 230–3) military doctrine suggest that military commanders may need to take the lead in tasks such as basic police training in country if the situation demands it.

So the very fact that military forces may be tasked with these activities — that official policy and doctrine make this a possibility — suggests that those doing the tasking are reasonably confident that military forces have the ability to perform these tasks in the first place. Note, too, that this attitude has also been encouraged by academic commentators, who have proposed that the widespread use of military for policing should be accepted as it is the 'least worst' option in circumstances where civilian police are either insufficient or unable to operate because of high levels of risk (Keller 2011; see also Mockaitis 2004, Jones et al. 2005 and Jayamaha et al. 2010 for similar suggestions). These wider societal attitudes would likely rub off on the military forces themselves, leading to the belief that they 'can do' these tasks if necessary.

As noted in Harding (this volume), this 'can do' attitude is also an integral part of the military identity. Although the primary role of infantry is 'to seek out and close with the enemy, to kill or capture him, to seize and hold ground, to repel attack, by day and night, regardless of season, weather or terrain' and each rifleman must be 'physically fit and healthy' as well as proficient at 'handling all Platoon weapons; fieldcraft; basic navigation; marksmanship; tracking; first aid; and the operation and maintenance of section specialist equipment' (NZ Army n.d.), infantry soldiers are also deployed to conduct other kinds of tasks.

The reason that army personnel may believe that they are capable of other tasks is that the military training they were given, and the sense of what it is to be a soldier that they gained there, was never reduced solely to the specific role of the infantry outlined above. As noted previously, taking on an overall soldier identity, which is not attached to any particular skill or occupational speciality, is a crucial element on which trainee soldiers are assessed and is key to the successful completion of their training. It is the focus of the first training course that new recruits must undergo — Basic Training — while specific roles such as that of the infantry above come afterwards in specialised 'Corps Training' courses.

Basic Training does teach basic infantry skills to soldiers of all occupations, but it is made clear to recruits that they are there to learn to 'display the qualities of a soldier' (again, see Harding, this volume). Recruits are required to 'self-lead' according to a set of common army values known by the acronym 3CI, consisting of Courage, Comradeship, Commitment and Integrity. Not only are these not related merely to traditional war-fighting, but they are also intended to be effective when applied to other types of tasks: soldiers are to self-lead according to these values not just on the job but also out in public, at home and in all spheres of life. These values should be 'the basis for your decision-making' (NZDF 2009c: 20) and 'must now serve as your guides when considering what is appropriate in any situation — whether you are in uniform or not' (NZDF 2009b: 2). Even in the case of the most obviously martial of the values, courage, it is repeatedly emphasised to recruits that courage is not meant to refer simply to physical courage under fire but also moral courage: 'strength of character to do what you know is right in spite of pressure to do something wrong' (NZ Army 2013: 14).

In defining what a soldier is and what therefore recruits are to work on becoming at Basic Training, the unit commander even expressly uses non-martial examples: soldiers are the guys at car crashes who don't just watch, but who jump in and help. If you turn up at the pub, and some guy is beating on his wife, it's the soldiers who step in rather than stand by. Military training, even for infantry, has not been designed solely for seeking out and closing with the enemy. It is designed so that whatever situation is encountered it is met with courage, commitment, comradeship and integrity and thus can be dealt with.

This has flow-on effects. Essentially there is enough ambiguity in training to suggest that military personnel may be able to undertake almost any role placed before them. This notion is backed up by other academic work such as that undertaken by Campbell and Campbell (2010), who contrasted the character, profile and work of personnel engaged in basic infantry (military) and constable (police) roles in the United States. Most interestingly for this chapter, they suggested that militaries, unlike police, do not focus on attitude adjustment when they are required to take on one another's role. Rather, they suggest, military personnel, when tasked with policing type roles, are more likely to focus on the acquisition of new skills. This may well be because, as noted above, soldiers have been socialised to have a certain attitude — or, to put it more strongly, a set of dispositions or identity characteristics — that is seen to be effective not only in martial situations but also in any situation in which civilian decision-makers may decide to place them.

So the basic training of military forces encourages them to see a new task such as policing as requiring not an attitude adjustment but rather the acquisition of new skills that can be applied alongside existing values. For example, soldiers have lessons in skills like the art of conversation, and in adjusting the body language in which they habitually hold themselves and their rifles during war-fighting exercises to something that feels less threatening to civilians. Acting on the values of 3CI (along with more informal dispositions that also make up the soldier identity, as discussed in Harding, this volume) prepares and aids soldiers to quickly learn new skills, on the job if necessary. In this way, as mentioned earlier, protection of the weak has been seen to be part of the soldier role since soldiers took this role on, and while academics may view engaging with civilians as a separate or even oppositional task to war-fighting, soldiers tend to see these as united in one skill set or identity. For example, Holmes-Eber (2014: 77) found that US Marines reconcile the roles of warrior and 'culturally aware counterinsurgent' through perceiving themselves as modern-day versions of chivalrous knights, while New Zealanders have consistently believed that their servicemen are 'good' soldiers because of a particular national character that is seen to allow them to empathise with, relate to and interact with others (see Harding, Morris, Lauren, Wineera and P. Greener, this volume).

The New Zealand Army is thus an institution which sees itself as inculcating a transposable soldier identity that can be applied in the field of combat, but also in other fields such as counterinsurgency, peacekeeping, disaster relief and so on. Given this transposable identity, therefore, we might assume that policing is simply yet another set of skills to be learned. If so, then learning these skills would potentially equip soldiers with the general ability to perform police tasks. As we saw above, the mere fact that military forces are not prevented from policing in high-threat situations does not show that they can, in fact, police those environments. For that to be the case, it would also have to be the case that they normally succeed when they try. So do they normally succeed? Well, that can only be evaluated against the backdrop of a clear notion of what successful attempts at policing look like.

The police perspective

THERE IS NO QUESTION THAT when a large-scale breakdown in social order occurs, through either natural or human causes, the deployment of resources to perform what would broadly be considered 'policing' tasks (such as patrol, static security and short-term detention) can have an immediate and successful impact in restoring overt security and stability. There is also little doubt, as is evidenced in places such as Timor-Leste and the Solomon Islands, that, as things stand, the New Zealand Army, and the NZDF more widely, has the capacity and capability to perform tasks of this kind. However, although the successful accomplishment of tasks such as these helps to establish an environment in which policing can begin to take place, successful 'policing' involves much more than this. For instance, in a September 2012 review of the New Zealand Police, key indicators of policing success include such intangible outcomes as being able to divert resources from responding to crime to prevention, having a victim-centred approach that significantly reduces victimisation and domestic violence, enabling communities to take the lead in problem solving, and working with other government agencies to reduce the drivers and opportunities for crime (State Services Commission et al. 2012: 18).

Could a military force succeed in performing tasks such as these by acquiring a range of new skills to apply alongside the transposable soldier values, as Campbell and Campbell described? There are reasons to be sceptical that this is possible. First, many policing skills are not the kind of skills that can be learned in the classroom, but are the kind of skills that not only need to be learned in the field but also need to be regularly honed and practised. For example, in order to succeed in preventing, rather than simply responding to, criminal activity, a police officer needs to be acutely sensitive to any departures from what is normal (Sacks 1972). To do this, police officers must first become highly familiar with the 'normal appearances' that characterise the areas they are responsible for policing, given that these normal appearances make up the 'background expectancies' against which the police officer looks for variations. As Sacks points out, however, this cannot be learned in the classroom but must be acquired through practical experience: 'The novice policeman is obviously not in a position to use the procedure. First he must learn how to see as a patrolman. By having a novice patrol with a mature officer, the former can be shown what it is that one can see by way of the method' (285). In addition to acquiring these skills in the field, they must also be regularly exercised:

> What is normal for a place is normal for the place at a time. The meaning of an event to the policeman at a place depends on the time it occurs. The time at which it occurs is furthermore a matter of an overlapping and changing group of cycles — that is, the meaning of an event is not merely a matter of the hour, but the day too is involved in deciding its significance; furthermore, the season counts, and then finally 'while it didn't used to be that way here,' now 'such a thing is typical' (286).

This suggests that only those who are regularly practising their policing skills — who are constantly 'policing' — will actually possess the kinds of skills required for the reliable successful performance of police tasks. Given that this is not a core role for members of military forces, they are unlikely to be able to devote the kind of time needed to policing tasks to successfully acquire and maintain the relevant skills.

In addition to this concern, it is also far from clear that the acquisition of skills alone will make the difference. As we saw above, and in Harding (this volume), to 'be' a soldier is to acquire a range of core values and dispositions — values of Courage, Commitment, Comradeship and Integrity — and to apply these values every day, in all of your decision-making, regardless of the situation you find yourself in. However, this is also true of what is required to 'be' a police officer, particularly as states evolve as liberal-democratic entities (see Greener and Fish 2015: 26–30). For example, where the New Zealand Army has the 3CI to provide the underlying basis of a soldier's decision-making, the New Zealand Police has a different set of values: the PRIMED values of professionalism, respect, integrity, commitment to Māori and the Treaty of Waitangi, empathy, and valuing diversity. The 2012 review suggests that to deliver the kinds of indicators of policing success identified above, police culture must embody and enact these policing values. This is reflected in the New Zealand Police Code of Conduct (2015), which talks repeatedly about 'living our values' (1, 3, 4), 'consciously exhibit[ing] behaviour that is aligned to our values' (2), and 'consistently demonstrating our values' (7). This is what it is to 'be' police. Just as to 'be' a soldier is to embody and enact a particular set of values in everything you do, to 'be' police is to embody and enact a different set of values. As a serving British police officer articulated in a group interview reported by Loftus (2010):

> It's not a job though is it? It's a lifestyle [others agree]. You can't go home and think, 'I am not a policeman.' You go home and you are who you are (5).

Successful policing is therefore not simply a matter of acquiring a range of new skills to apply alongside existing values (even if it were possible — given the concerns described above — to acquire those skills in the first place). To successfully perform policing tasks, soldiers would also need to acquire and embody a different set of values — that is, they would need to *become* police.

So while military forces can and do play a critical role in the establishment and support of a functional policing environment in post-conflict scenarios, the same forces cannot be expected to successfully police those environments. Once an initial level of stability has been restored, a range of complex law enforcement issues often follows, from the black economies that form during humanitarian disasters to the criminality and impunity that is born out of post-conflict theatres. These are complicated, and often long-term, problems that can only be addressed by a strong internal security sector, including police, justice and corrections. And only police — that is, only actors who have embodied the appropriate values and developed the appropriate skills — can successfully perform these policing tasks. Only trained and dedicated police, therefore, have the general ability to perform police tasks. The overarching explanation of why soldiers cannot successfully perform policing roles is thus relatively simple: they are not police.

Generalising, the underlying claim here is that, while there may well be many practical and technical abilities that military forces can successfully acquire by learning new skills to apply alongside their core military values, there is a range of abilities that cannot be acquired in this way. In asking whether military forces can acquire an ability in this fashion, then, there are two key questions to ask. First, do those who have the ability in question have to acquire (and cultivate) that skill through practical experience (and regular performance)? Second, do those who have the ability in question have this ability, at least in part, in virtue of their acquisition and embodiment of particular professional values?

If the answer to either of these questions is yes, then the military's approach to upskilling is unlikely to be successful. As to the first, to the extent that the acquisition and maintenance of a particular ability requires regular performance, the acquisition of such an ability would (as the soldiers interviewed by Greener and Fish feared) have a negative effect on their core military operational capacity. As to the second, to the extent that a soldier's identity as a soldier is a matter of the particular core values and dispositions that they embody, acquiring an alternative set of values and dispositions would not leave their identity as a soldier unaffected.

Communicating the limits of the military

IF THE NATURE OF MILITARY forces means that they will lack the general ability to perform certain tasks, then — if we follow von Clausewitz —

it is incumbent upon the military to make this clear to their political masters. We might worry, however, that this is a precarious thing to embolden military forces to do: If we start allowing military forces to choose what to do and what not to do, where will it end? This takes us to the heart of the challenge of civil–military relations: 'to reconcile a military strong enough to do anything the civilians ask them to with a military subordinate enough to do *only* what civilians authorise them to do' (Feaver 1996: 149, our emphasis). The influential civil–military scholar Samuel P. Huntington (1957) argues that to maximise military security — that is, to find the ideal equilibrium between maximising military power and minimising military threat — we should not attempt to ground civilian control in external constraints on military behaviour through maximising the power of civilian groups in relation to the military, but should rather focus on the attitudes within the military itself.

Key to this approach is inculcating within the military forces a professional culture that will lead the military to voluntarily place itself under civilian control. In such a system, the 'statesmen set the goal and allocate . . . the resources to be used in attaining that goal. It is then up to [the military officer] to do the best he can . . . When the military man receives a legal order from an authorised superior, he does not argue, he does not hesitate, he does not substitute his own views; he obeys instantly' (72–3). This might lead us to think that the price we pay for ensuring that military forces stay out of politics and civilian affairs is that they cannot be allowed to question their civilian authorities. Given this, we might think that it is not only inappropriate but also dangerous to encourage military forces to 'answer back' when they are given a particular task by the state. Instead, they should just — as they have been doing since the 1990s — accept the role they have been tasked with, and try their best to perform it as successfully as possible.

It is important to note, however, that for Huntington the *executive* function — the responsibility of the military to implement state decisions

— is not the only responsibility that military officers have to the state. In addition to this responsibility, Huntington claims that military officers also have an advisory function, and it is in the performance of this function that the military should inform policy-makers about the limits of the military instrument: 'If the state leaders are weighing three possible policies, the military man, of course, cannot judge which is the most desirable. He may, however, say that . . . [a] policy is simply beyond the military capacity of the state to implement effectively' (ibid.: 52). What is more, even where the executive function is concerned, Huntington allows that a subordinate may, in such cases, make his views and concerns known to his superior, so long as he obeys if the superior persists in that order (see the discussion at 75). So even on a view such as Huntington's — which focuses on the attitudes within the military itself — military commanders advising their political masters on what they can and cannot do is not deemed to be in conflict with the desire for civilian control of the military.

This structure — of civilian authority coupled with military advice — can be seen in the way the New Zealand government makes decisions about defence matters. Although the Governor-General is nominally Commander-in-Chief of the NZDF and thus 'constitutionally the supreme authority in defence matters in New Zealand' (NZDF n.d.), the Governor-General only exercises power on the advice of the Minister of Defence and other ministers, and 'executive power of control [. . .] is vested in the Cabinet, which exercises authority over the armed forces through the minister' (MoD/NZDF 2005: 38). Thus, when it comes to deploying military forces, the ultimate decision-making authority rests with the prime minister with approval by Cabinet (although there is no legal requirement to obtain Parliament's consent, this has nonetheless typically been the practice) (New Zealand Parliament 2014). However, prior to exercising this authority, the prime minister and Cabinet solicit advice from those who undertake action. Coordination of a range of advice from across government sectors is provided through the Officials Committee for Defence and External Security Coordination (ODESC). ODESC brings together representatives from different agencies depending upon the situation, and is charged with providing cross-ministerial strategic policy advice on all security and intelligence matters.

The NZDF is the sole provider of armed forces to the New Zealand government (NZDF 2009a: 10; ibid. 2010: 11). The primary legislation governing defence is the Defence Act 1990, the key functions of which are to 'continue to authorise the raising and maintaining of armed forces for certain purposes', 'constitute the NZDF' and to 'reaffirm that the Armed Forces are under Ministerial authority' (Defence Act 1990: 6). In terms of the specifics of military responsibilities under the act, the Ministry of Defence is responsible for formulating defence policy, procuring major equipment, and auditing and assessing the defence force (NZDF 2009a; 2010). The chief executive of the Ministry of Defence is the Secretary of Defence, who is the principal civilian advisor to the minister. Through Part 1 section 7 of the Defence Act the Minister of Defence has the power of control of the NZDF, with this power of control being exercised through the Chief of Defence Force (CDF). However, the minister clearly relies upon the specialist advice provided by the CDF in making decisions, as the CDF is the minister's principal military advisor. Importantly, too, the minister may delegate to the CDF any of the minister's powers, duties or functions (ibid.) — having the potential to allow the minister to abdicate varying degrees of responsibility.

The recent deployment to Iraq (discussed in Wineera, this volume) demonstrates the process of approving military deployments. Following a request for help from the Iraqi government, Cabinet originally approved an initial scoping mission to ascertain how New Zealand might help the Iraqi Army counter the threat of ISIL/Daesh (ibid.). In light of this, and with advice from then CDF Tim Keating that the experience of the NZDF in providing high-quality military training programmes would be valuable, Cabinet then agreed that (subject to the agreement of ministers with the power to act — the prime minister, deputy prime minister, ministers of defence and foreign affairs, and the attorney-general) New Zealand would make a military contribution of 106 personnel for an initial period of two years (ibid.). Provided that it did not significantly increase the deployment numbers or alter the cost or intent of the mission, Cabinet also 'authorised the Minister of Defence, in consultation with the Minister of Foreign Affairs, to make adjustments to the deployment in response to operational requirements' (ibid.).

In discussing his role in providing advice on this matter, Keating emphasised the issues of risk and value in undertaking the deployment:

> As the government's principal military advisor, I weighed up the likely outcomes and the risks of supporting the international coalition against the Islamic State in Iraq and the Levant (ISIL) . . . We have a track record of providing quality military training. This is where we are again going to make a difference. Although this is not a combat mission, we recognise the inherent risks of sending our personnel to Iraq. I assure our personnel and their families that we will do everything possible to ensure their safety (Keating 2015a).

Keating further stated that, as CDF, 'I have had to satisfy myself as to what we can achieve, and what the risks are of deploying our men and women on this training mission', also noting that, following consultation with other senior defence and security advisors, 'I have formed the view that this is a mission *within the capabilities of the New Zealand Defence Force*' (Keating 2015b, emphasis added). This example demonstrates how senior military advisors may seek to evaluate capacity and then advise political decision-makers — explicitly referring to the need to be able to perform the task and balance risk, and to the value-added nature of military deployments.

Lessons for military engagement

AS WE HAVE SEEN, TO have the (particular) ability to perform a specific task is to have the general ability to perform tasks of that kind — that is, to be reliably successful when attempting tasks of that kind — and for there to be nothing that prevents success on this particular occasion. We have already seen that, in post-conflict environments, civilian police forces lack the ability to police as they are prevented by the inherent level of danger. Our discussions also suggest that military forces also lack the ability to police in these environments, not because they are prevented but because they lack the general ability to perform (the bulk of) police tasks in the first place. This suggests two ways forward: either to provide military forces with the general ability (without thereby rendering them prevented) or to find ways of removing the impediments from civilian police forces (without thereby denying them the general ability). Both of these options seem worth exploring.

In order for the military to acquire the general ability to perform more aspects of the police role, we have seen that they would not only have to train differently — in that they would need to be given opportunities to not only acquire but also to practise police skills — but they would also need to adopt a different set of core values and dispositions. As we have noted, this would have an unavoidable impact on the forces themselves in that they would have to become somewhat different from what we consider to be a traditional military force. The military establishment would become hybridised — what Janowitz calls a 'constabulary force' — a force that is 'continuously prepared to act, committed to the minimum use of force, and seeks viable international relations, rather than victory' (1960: 418). For the New Zealand Army to become this kind of constabulary force, it would need to become even more individualised, humanised and 'legalised' (Greener 2007) in approach than it currently is. This is not inconceivable, however: there are precedents in New Zealand's actions in the past, such as the decision by the New Zealand Army to deploy an unarmed operation as part of the military contingent (see Stevens and Greener, this volume), which might indicate the potential to move in this direction.

However, the emphasis in the international environment on military forces as integral to the sovereignty and status of states makes this task very difficult. Defence diplomacy requires interoperability with other military forces. Having air, sea and land assets to bring to coalition operations is important for contemporary statecraft. And, finally, the argument remains that combat might be necessary given the fact that internationally others have adhered to this norm of utilising military force and forces in certain circumstances. Given these issues, then, the time may not yet be ripe for transforming the army into 'something else'. And there is another option to consider that might be more readily achievable.

As we have seen, the main impediments to using police abroad are those related to difficulties in deploying police in the first place, and the dangers involved in deploying police to hostile environments. In terms of addressing these shortfalls (discussed in detail in Greener and Fish 2015: chapters 7 and 8), some countries have recognised the need for a 'whole of government' approach and have explored how to facilitate the use of agencies other than the military. Yet the capabilities needed to send civilians or police to overseas operations remain inadequate. Attempts have been made to get around these limitations by the creation of civilian reserve corps (such as that in Australia, which aims to be able to deploy 800 civilians from a wide range of backgrounds) and, in some countries, international policing deployment groups (again, Australia has experimented with a deployment group of up to 1200 police able to deploy internationally, even supported by their own helicopters and other infrastructure).

In New Zealand, however, the NZDF is not yet able to call on such well-established and well-resourced civilian agencies, which means that the support it receives is piecemeal: the Ministry of Foreign Affairs provided individuals to the Solomon Islands and (towards the end of the mission) to lead the Provincial Reconstruction Team in Afghanistan; New Zealand Police have been involved with a number of deployments but, despite having had an International Services Group since 2005, they have no consistent budget stream for this group, nor do they have a pool of police officers trained and waiting to deploy overseas; individuals from Inland Revenue or the Treasury or the health services may be requested to deploy overseas, but again there is no standing capacity in play, nor is there a civilian reserve corps. Given the limits of the military instrument when it comes to tasks such as policing in peace and stability operations, military commanders need additional external sources of support: they may be able to say 'we cannot' more if there are others who are able to say 'we can'.

Conclusion

THIS CHAPTER DRAWS THE BOOK as a whole to a close. Reflecting on what the military is may also be rendered more clearly by considering what it is not. At the present time the New Zealand Army is becoming more gender aware, more interested in education and training, less emphatic about rote learning and — perhaps most fundamentally, as raised in a number of chapters herein — more focused on 'professionalism' as a key trait. Soldiers and officers may have different expectations of what is involved, as may different generations of these personnel. Men and women may have different experiences in their engagement with the military. The recent emphasis on development and conflict resolution has raised questions about the suitability of the military instrument to solve all ills. Yet positive views of the New Zealand Army generally predominate, and this text highlights the ability of military institutions to adapt to a certain degree. However, as other government agencies jostle for ever-dwindling funds, it will be important to mark out what the purpose of the New

Zealand Defence Force really is — a purpose that will only be discerned by constant and critical assessment of how demands are changing and, in particular, by an honest evaluation of the limits of the military instrument in responding to those demands.

References

ABC News (2013). Chief of Army David Morrison tells troops to respect women or 'get out'. http://www.abc.net.au/news/2013-06-14/chief-of-army-fires-broadside-at-army-over-email-allegations/4753208

—— (2014). Defence 'making significant progress' in improving gender culture, sex discrimination commissioner finds. http://www.abc.net.au/news/2014-03-26/elizabeth-broderick-report-on-women-in-defence/5347120

—— (2015). Create the society you want to live in, urges Chief of Army. http://www.abc.net.au/news/2015-05-11/create-the-society-you-want-to-live-in-urges-chief/6461784

Accord Insight (2013). *Women Building Peace.* Conciliation Resources: London.

Ackerly, B., M. Stern and J. True (2006). *Feminist Methodologies for International Relations.* Cambridge: Cambridge University Press.

Adams, R., ed. (2001). Peace on Bougainville — Truce Monitoring Group, Gudpela Nius Bilong Peace. Wellington: Victoria University Press.

Al Jazeera (2016). 'Sickening' sex abuse alleged in CAR by UN peacekeepers. http://www.aljazeera.com/news/2016/03/ sex-abuse-alleged-car-peacekeepers-160331183645566.html, accessed 3 May 2016.

Amnesty International (2001). Massacres in Yakaolang. https://www.hrw.org/reports/2001/afghanistan/afghan101-03.htm#P126_15001, accessed July 2016.

Ankersen, C. (2008). Introduction: Interrogating Civil–Military Cooperation. In *Civil-Military Cooperation in Post Conflict Operations: Emerging theory and practice,* ed. C. Ankerson. Abingdon: Routledge.

Ansary, T. (2014). Games without Rules: The often-interrupted history of Afghanistan. New York: Public Affairs.

Anson, D. (2005). Extending the Push for Peace: The New Zealand Defence Force in action. In *Push for Peace,* ed. P. Greener, pp. 26–31. Auckland: Auckland University of Technology and Auckland War Memorial Museum.

Association of Social Anthropologists of the UK and the Commonwealth (1999). Ethical Guidelines for Good Research Practice. http://www.theasa.org/downloads/ethics/Ethical_guidelines.pdf, accessed July 2016.

Austrian Development Cooperation (2009). Focus: Women, gender and armed conflict. http://www.oecd.org/dac/gender-development/44896284.pdf

Avery, D. R., and P. F. McKay (2006). Target practice: An organizational impression management approach to attracting minority and female job applicants. *Personnel Psychology*, Vol. 59, No. 1, pp. 157–187.

Ayson, R. (2004). New Zealand: Armed to make a difference? In *Forces for Good? Cosmopolitan militaries in the 21st century*, ed. L. Elliott and G. Cheeseman, pp. 250–262. Manchester: Manchester University Press.

Baguioro, L. (2016). NZ and Australian troops teach Iraqi soldiers basic lifesaving skills. *NZ Army News*, No. 469, p. 9.

Barany, Z. (2012). *The Soldier and the Changing State: Building democratic armies in Africa, Asia, Europe and the Americas.* Princeton NJ: Princeton University Press.

Barsh, J., S. Nudelman and L. Yee (2013). Lessons from the leading edge of gender diversity. *McKinsey Quarterly*, April. http://www.mckinsey.com/insights/organization/lessons_ from_the_leading_edge_of_gender_diversity

Bednar, A. K., D. Cunningham, T. M. Duffy and J. P. Perry (1995). Theory into practice: How do we link? In *Instructional technology: Past, present and future*, 2nd ed., ed. G. J. Anglin, pp. 100–111. Englewood, CO: Libraries Unlimited, Inc.

Bennett, J. (2003). 'Massey's Sunday School Picnic Party': 'The Other Anzacs' or honorary Australians? *War & Society*, Vol. 21, No. 2, pp. 23–54.

—— (2009). The Softer Side of Security. *ISN Security Watch*, 1 July. http://www.isn.ethz.ch/isn/Current-Affairs/Security-Watch/Detail/?ots591= 4888CAA0-B3DB-1461-98B9-E20E7B9C13D4&lng=en&id=102726, accessed 1 August 2009.

Betts Fetherston, A. (1998). Voices from Warzones: Implications for training UN peacekeepers. In *A Future for Peacekeeping?*, ed. E. Moxon-Browne. Basingstoke: Macmillan.

Birzer, M. L. (2003). The theory of andragogy applied to police training. *Policing: An international journal of police strategies & management*, Vol. 26, No. 1, pp. 29–42.

Boas, M., and K. M. Jennings (2005). Insecurity and Development: The rhetoric of the failed state. *European Journal of Development Research*, Vol. 17, No. 3, pp. 385–395.

Boesveld, S. (2014). Young children already buy into gender stereotypes to explain behaviour in fairytales: study. *National Post Canada*, 27 May. http://news.nationalpost.com/news/canada/young-children-already-buy-into-gender-stereotypes-to-explain-behaviour-in-fairy-tales-study

Bojilova, A. (2013). Observing through ambiguity: The countless sources of stress in the ever-changing face of the UNTSO Golan Mission . . . *Golan – The UNDOF Journal*, No. 135, p. 19.

Bondy, H. (2005). Personality type and military culture in the Anglo-West. *Australian Defence Force Journal*, Vol. 10, No. 169, pp. 4–14.

Bourdieu, P. (1977). *Outline of a theory of practice*, trans. R. Nice. Cambridge: Cambridge University Press.

—— (1990). *The logic of practice*, trans. R. Nice. Cambridge: Polity Press.

Bourdieu, P., and J. C. Passeron (1990). *Reproduction in education, society and culture*, trans. R. Nice, 2nd ed. London: Sage Publications.

Bridges, D., and D. Horsfall (2009). Increasing Operational Effectiveness in UN Peacekeeping: Toward a gender-balanced force. *Armed Forces and Society*, Vol. 36, No. 1, pp. 120–130.

Brooke, M. (2005). Op Anode Deters Criminal Elements. *Army: The Soldier's Newspaper*, 3 November, www.defence.gov.au/news/armynews/editions/1132/topstories/story20a.htm

Brookfield, S. (1986). *Understanding and Facilitating Adult Learning: A comprehensive analysis of principles and effective practices*. San Francisco CA: Jossey-Bass.

Bruneau, T., and F. Matei, eds (2013). *Routledge Handbook of Civil–Military Relations*. London and New York: Routledge.

Bruno, G. (2010). Afghanistan's National Security Forces. Council for Foreign Relations. http://www.cfr.org/afghanistan/afghanistans-national-security-forces/p19122, accessed 2 April 2015.

Buchbinder, D. (1994). *Masculinities and Identities*. Melbourne: Melbourne University Press.

Burke, C. (2004). *Camp All-American, Hanoi Jane and the high-and-tight: Gender, folklore, and changing military culture*. Boston: Beacon Press.

Burton, C. (1998). *Report of the Gender Integration Audit of the New Zealand Defence Force*. New Zealand Defence Force and New Zealand Human Rights Commission.

Butler, J. (1990). *Gender Trouble: Feminism and the Subversion of Identity*. New York: Routledge.

Caffarella, R. S. (1993). Self-directed learning. In S. Merriam (ed.), *New Directions for Adult and Continuing Education* No. 57, pp. 25–35. San Francisco CA: Jossey-Bass.

Caforio, G., ed. (2003). *Handbook of the Sociology of the Military*. New York: Kluwer Academic.

—— ed. (2007). *Social Sciences and the Military: An interdisciplinary overview*. London: Routledge.

Campbell, D. J., and K. M. Campbell (2010). Soldiers as Police Officers/Police Officers as Soldiers: Role evolution and revolution in the United States. *Armed Forces and Society*, Vol. 36, No. 2, pp. 327–350.

Carreiras, H., and A. Alexandre (2013). Research relations in military settings: How does gender matter? In *Qualitative Methods in Military Studies*, ed. H. C. C. Castro, pp. 97–116. Abingdon, Routledge.

Carter, B. L. (2010). No Holidays from History: Adult learning, professional military education, and teaching history. In *Military education and culture*, ed. D. Higbee, pp. 167–182. Surrey: Ashgate.

Channa, J. (2002). Security Sector Reform: Issues, challenges and prospects. *Adelphi Papers* 344. London: International Institute for Strategic Studies.

Charlesworth, Hilary (2008). Are Women Peaceful? Reflections on the role of women in peace-building. *Feminist Legal Studies*, Vol. 16, No. 3, pp. 347–361.

Chief of Navy (2014). Making our navy a safer and healthier workplace. http://www.navy.mil.nz/nap/nn/20141008-cnwad.htm

Chinkin, C., and H. Charlesworth (2006). Building Women into Peace: The international legal framework. *Third World Quarterly*, Vol. 27, No. 5, pp. 937–957. http://www.ceipaz.org/images/contenido/peacebuilding2.pdf

Clarke, N. (2003). The politics of training needs analysis. *Journal of Workplace Learning*, Vol. 15, No. 4, pp. 141–153.

von Clausewitz, C. (1976). *On War*, ed. and trans. M. Howard and P. Paret. Princeton NJ: Princeton University Press.

—— (1984). *Two Letters on Strategy*, ed. and trans. P. Paret and D. Moran. Reprinted by the Combat Studies Institute, Fort Leavenworth KS. http://usacac.army.mil/cac2/cgsc/carl/download/csipubs/carlvonc.pdf, accessed 5 June 2015.

Clements, K. P., V. Boege, W. Foley and W. Nolan (2007). State Building Reconsidered: The role of hybridity in the formation of political order. *Political Science*, Vol. 59, No. 1, pp. 45–56.

Cobane, C. T. (2005). Provincial Reconstruction Teams and Security Assistance: Comments on an evolving concept. *DISAM Journal of International Security Cooperation Management*, Vol. 27, No. 4, pp. 91–97.

Code Blue (2016). Media Highlights: Reports of sexual abuse by Canadian peacekeepers in Haiti. http://www.codebluecampaign.com /latest-news/2016/8/1-1, accessed 3 August 2016.

Cohen, E. A. (1995). *Citizens and Soldiers: The dilemmas of military service.* Ithaca NY: Cornell University Press.

—— (2002). *Supreme Command: Soldiers, statesmen, and leadership in wartime.* New York: Free Press.

Coleman, J., and M. McCully (2013). New Zealand to maintain support as Afghanistan mission transitions. http://www.beehive.govt.nz/release/NewZealand-maintain-support-afghanistan-mission-transitions, accessed 29 October 2014.

Collins, M. (1991). *Adult Education as Vocation: A critical role for the adult educator.* New York and London: Routledge.

Cordesman, A. H., with A. Mausner (2007). Iraqi Force Development: Conditions for success, consequences of failure. *CSIS Report.* Washington DC: Center for Strategic and International Studies.

Cotton, J. (1995). *The Theory of Learning: An introduction.* London: Kogan Page.

Cowen, M. P., and R. W. Shenton (1996). *Doctrines of Development.* London: Routledge.

Coyne, C. J. (2006). Reconstructing Weak and Failed States: Foreign intervention and the nirvana fallacy. *Foreign Policy Analysis*, Vol. 2, No. 4, pp. 343–360.

Crawford, J. (1996). *In the Field for Peace: New Zealand's contribution to international peace-support operations: 1950–1995.* Wellington: NZDF.

Crawford, J., and G. Harper (2001). *Operation East Timor: The New Zealand Defence Force in East Timor 1999–2001.* Auckland: Reed.

van Creveld, M. (2000). Armed But Not Dangerous: Women in the Israeli military. *War in History*, Vol. 7, No. 1, pp. 82–98.

Dandeker, C. (2010). From Victory to Success: The changing mission of Western armed forces. In *Modern War and the Utility of Force,* ed. J. Angstrom and I. Duvesteyn, pp. 16–38. London: Routledge.

Davidson, M. J. (1999). *A Guide to Military Criminal Law: A practical guide for all the services.* Annapolis: Naval Institute Press.

Desch, M. (2001). *Civilian Control of the Military: The changing security environment.* Baltimore MA: Johns Hopkins University.

Donald, H. (2005). *In Peace and War: A civilian soldier's story.* Masterton: Fraser Books.

Donoghue, J., and B. Tranter (2015). The Anzacs: Military influences on Australian identity. *Journal of Sociology*, Vol. 51, No. 3, pp. 449–463.

Downes, C. (2000). Australia and New Zealand: Contingent and concordant militaries. In *The Postmodern Military: Armed forces after the cold war*, ed. C. Moskos, J. A. Williams and D. R. Segal. Oxford: Oxford University Press.

Dransfield, M. (2016). Perspectives on the Challenges, Opportunities and Imperatives for Mission Success in Afghanistan and Timor-Leste. In *United Nations Peacekeeping Challenge: The importance of an integrated approach*, ed. A. Powles, N. Partow and N. Nelson, pp. 57–72. London and New York: Routledge.

Duffield, M. (2005). Getting Savages to Fight Barbarians: Development, security and the colonial present. *Conflict, Security and Development*, Vol. 5, No. 2, pp. 141–159.

Duncanson, C. (2009). Forces for Good? Narratives of Military Masculinity in Peacekeeping Operations. *International Feminist Journal of Politics,* Vol. 11, No. 1, pp. 63–80.

—— (2013). *Forces for Good? Military masculinities and peacebuilding in Afghanistan and Iraq.* Houndmills: Palgrave.

Duxfield, J. (2012). New Zealand on the Ground in Afghanistan: A personal view. In Legacy of Armistice — why Afghanistan? Lecture at AUT and the Auckland War Memorial Museum.

Dziedzic, M. J., and M. K. Seidl (2005). *Provincial Reconstruction Teams and Military Relations with International and Nongovernmental Organisations in Afghanistan.* Washington DC: United States Institute of Peace. http://www.usip.org/publications/provincial-reconstruction-teams-military-relations-international-and-nongovernmental

Earp, R. (2016). *Building Partner Capacity, an Afghan Experience.* Unpublished staff paper.

Edmund, T. (2006). What *are* armed forces for? The changing nature of military roles in Europe. *International Affairs,* Vol. 82, No. 6, pp. 1059–1075.

Egnell, R. (2008). Between reluctance and necessity: The utility of military force in humanitarian and development operations. *Small Wars & Insurgencies,* Vol. 19, No. 3, pp. 397–422.

—— (2009). *Complex Peace Operations and Civil-Military Relations: Winning the peace.* London and New York: Routledge.

—— (2013). Women in Battle: Gender perspectives and fighting. Carlisle PA: Strategic Studies Institute. http://www.strategicstudiesinstitute.army.mil/pubs/Parameters/issues/ Summer_2013/4_ Egnell_Article.pdf.

Eizenstat, S., J. Porter and J. Weinstein (2005). Rebuilding Weak States. *Foreign Affairs,* Vol. 84, No. 1, pp. 134–146. New York NY: Council on Foreign Relations.

Enloe, C. (1983). *Does Khaki Become You?* Boston: South End Press.

—— (1989). *Bananas, Beaches and Bases: Making feminist sense of international politics.* Berkley CA: University of California Press.

—— (2000). *Maneuvers: The international politics of militarizing women's lives.* Los Angeles CA: University of California Press.

—— (2007). *Globalisation and Militarism: Feminists make the link.* Lanham MD: Rowman and Littlefield.

Evans, M. (2010). *Captains of the Soul: Stoic philosophy and the Western profession of arms in the twenty-first century,* p. 45. http://www.defence.gov.au/ADC/Docs/CDLE/ CDLE_120329_EvansM2010CaptainsoftheSoul.pdf

Feaver, P. (1996). The Civil–Military Problematique: Huntington, Janowitz, and the question of civilian control. *Armed Forces and Society,* Vol. 23, No. 2, pp. 149–178.

—— (2003). *Armed Servants: Agency, oversight, and civil-military relations.* Harvard: Harvard University Press.

Fellows, J. (2005). Why Iraq has no Army. *The Atlantic.* http://www. theatlantic.com/

magazine/archive/2005/12/why-iraq-has-no-army/304428/, accessed 15 February 2016.

Fepulea'i, J. (2010). RAMSI and Solomon Islands: History and challenges for civil-military interaction. Asia Pacific Civil Military Centre of Excellence Working Paper No. 4. Queanbeyan: Asia Pacific Civil Military Centre of Excellence.

Finer, S. (1962). *The Man on Horseback: The role of the military in politics.* London: Pall Mall Press.

Forde, R. (1998). Army grads are first from new course. *Manawatu Standard,* 23 May, p. 8.

Forster, A. (2006). Breaking the Covenant: Governance of the British Army in the twenty-first century. *International Affairs,* Vol. 82, No. 6, pp. 1043–1057.

Frankel, J. (2004). *The Manipulation of Kastom: From uprising to intervention in the Solomon Islands.* Wellington: Victoria University Press.

du Fresne, K. (2014). No big surprise that military not a happy place for women. *Dominion Post,* 21 February.

—— (2015). Fighting talk. *NZ Listener,* June. http://www.listener.co.nz/current-affairs/foreign-affairs/fighting-talk-2/

Friesendorf, C. (2009). *The Military and Law Enforcement in Peace Operations.* Frankfurt: Geneva Centre for the Democratic Control of Armed Forces.

Gagné, R. (1962). Military training and principles of learning. *American Psychologist,* Vol. 17, pp. 263–276.

—— (1974). *Essentials of Learning and Instruction.* Hinsdale: Dryden Press.

—— (1985). *The Conditions of Learning,* 4th ed. New York: Holt, Rinehart and Winston.

Gagné, R. M., and L. J. Briggs (1974). *Principles of Instructional Design.* New York: Holt, Rinehart and Winston.

Gagné, R. M., and W. Dick (1983). Instructional psychology. *Annual Review of Psychology,* Vol. 34, No. 1, pp. 261–295.

Gagné, R. M., and K. L. Medsker (1996). *The Conditions of Learning: Training Applications.* Fort Worth: Harcourt Brace College Publishers.

Gates, R. M. (2007). Speech by Secretary of Defense Robert M. Gates to the Association of the United States Army, October 10, US Department of Defense, Washington DC. http://www.defenselink.mil/speeches, accessed 27 January.

—— (2010). Helping others defend themselves: the future of US security assistance. *Foreign Affairs,* 2–6.

Gawn, D. (2010). Helping Others Defend Themselves: The Future of U.S. Security Assistance. *Foreign Afffairs,* Vol. 89, No. 3, pp. 2–6.

—— (2015). A Message from Chief of Army: Women in conflict. *NZ Army News*, No. 461, p. 3.

Genat, A., Prof. R. Wood and Dr V. Sojo (2014). *Evaluation Bias and Backlash: Dimensions, predictions and implications for organisations* (programme published for the Gender Equality Project). Centre for Ethical Leadership, Melbourne Business School.

Gilbert, N. (2008). Research, theory and method. In *Researching social life*, 3rd ed., ed. N. Gilbert. London: Sage Publications.

Gill, Z. W. (2009). Rehearsing the War Away: Perpetual warrior training in contemporary US Army policy. *Drama Review*, Vol. 53, No. 3, pp. 139–155.

Glenn, R. (2007). *Counter-Insurgency in a Test Tube: Analyzing the success of the regional assistance mission to Solomon Islands (RAMSI)*. Santa Monica CA: RAND.

Goldsmith, A., and V. Harris (2010). Police–military cooperation in foreign interventions: Timor-Leste and the Solomon Islands. In *International Police Cooperation: Emerging issues, theory and practice*, ed. F. Lemieux, pp. 221–240. Devon and Portland OR: Willan Publishing.

—— (2011). Out of step: multilateral police missions, culture and nation-building in Timor-Leste. In *Security, Development and Nation-Building in Timor-Leste: A cross-sectoral assessment*, ed. V. Harris and A. Goldsmith. pp. 162–182. New York: Routledge.

Goldstein, J. (2001). *War and Gender*, 2nd ed. Cambridge: Cambridge University Press.

Goodson, L. P. (2001). *Afghanistan's Endless War*. Seattle: University of Washington Press.

Green, S. (2012). Fairy Tales and Gender Stereotypes. *The Huffington Post*. http://www.huffingtonpost.com/samara-green/fairy-tales-and-gender-st_b_1273872.html

Greener, B. K. (2007). Liberalism, Liberal States and Military Force. *Global Change, Peace and Security*, Vol. 19, No. 2, pp. 67–81.

Greener, B. K., and W. J. Fish (2011). *The Development of Civilian Policing: Lessons for Contemporary Post Conflict Operations*. Civil–Military Occasional Paper 4/2011. Queanbeyan: Asia Pacific Civil Military Centre of Excellence.

—— (2015). *Internal Security and Statebuilding: Aligning agencies and functions*. London and New York: Routledge.

Greener, B. K., W. J. Fish and K. Tekulu (2011). Peacebuilding, Gender and Policing in Solomon Islands. *Asia Pacific Viewpoint*, Vol. 52, No. 1 (April), pp. 17–28.

Greener, B. K., and A. Powles (2015). *The 'sons – and daughters – of ANZAC'?*

Australian Strategic Policy Institute. http://www.aspistrategist.org.au/the-sons-and-daughters-of-anzac/

Greener, P. (2009). *Timing is Everything: The politics and processes of New Zealand defence acquisition.* Canberra: Strategic and Defensive Studies Centre series, Australian National University Press.

—— (2012). Introduction. In *Sinai Journal: 30 Years of Kiwis serving with the Multinational Force and Observers*, ed. S. Chandler and C. O'Hara-Smith. Wellington: NZDF/Te Ope Kaatua o Aotearoa in association with Willson Scott International.

Greig, A. (2006). Lebanon: A personal view of the conflict. *Air Force News*, No. 74, pp. 10–11.

Gulliver, A. (2015). Low female Defence Force recruit numbers 'disturbing'. http://www.stuff.co.nz/national/politics/67645891/Low-female-Defence-Force-recruit-numbers-disturbing

Hage, G. (2013). Eavesdropping on Bourdieu's philosophers. *Thesis Eleven*, Vol. 114, No. 1, pp. 76–93.

Hall, R. (2010). *A Long Road to Progress: Dispatches from a Kiwi commander in Afghanistan.* Auckland: Random House.

Hammersley, M., and P. Atkinson (2007). *Ethnography: Principles in practice*, 3rd ed. London: Routledge.

Harding, N. J. (2008). Composing the War: Nation and self in narratives of the Royal New Zealand Air Force deployment to the 1991 Gulf conflict. Master's thesis, University of Canterbury, Christchurch.

Harper, G. (2011). New Zealand's Vietnam War: A history of combat, commitment and controversy. *Journal of Military History*, Vol. 75, No. 1, pp. 334–336.

—— (2012). *Massacre at Passchendaele: The New Zealand story.* London and Auckland: HarperCollins.

—— (2015). *Dark Journey: Passchendaele, the Somme and the New Zealand experience on the Western Front.* Auckland: HarperCollins.

——— (2016). The New Zealand soldier of the First World War 14–15: Johnny Enzed. In *Experience of a Lifetime: People, Personalities and Leaders in the First World War*), ed. J. Crawford, D. Littlewood and J. Watson, pp. 62–82. Auckland: Massey University Press.

Harris, V., and A. Goldsmith (2010). Gendering Transnational Policing: Experiences of Australian women in international policing operations. *International Peacekeeping*, Vol. 17, No. 2, pp. 292–306.

Hayward, A. (2003). *East Timor: A case study in humanitarian intervention.* New

Zealand Army Military Studies Institute Occasional Paper Series, Wellington: Military Studies Institute.

Hennigan, W. J. (2016). US shifts troops in the Sinai Peninsula after attacks by militants. *Los Angeles Times*, 23 April. http://www.latimes.com/world/middleeast/la-fg-us-sinai-20160423-story.html, accessed 1 June 2016.

Higate, P. (2007). Peacekeepers, Masculinities and Sexual Exploitation. *Men and Masculinities*, Vol. 10, No. 1, pp. 99–119.

—— (2011). 'Cowboys and Professionals': The politics of identity work in the private and military security company. *Millennium — Journal of International Studies*, Vol. 40, No. 2, pp. 321–341.

—— (2015). Aversions to Masculine Excess in the Private Military and Security Company and their Effects: Don't be a 'Billy Big Bollocks' and 'Beware the Ninja'. In *Gender and Private Security in Global Politics*, ed. M. Eichler, pp. 131–45. Oxford: Oxford University Press.

Higate, P., and A. Cameron (2006). Reflexivity and Researching the Military. *Armed Forces & Society*, Vol. 32, No. 2, pp. 219–233.

Higate, P., and M. Henry (2004). Engendering (In)security in Peace Support Operations. *Security Dialogue*, Vol. 35, No. 4 (December), pp. 481–498.

Higgins, K. (2008). *Outside In: A volunteer's reflections on a Solomon Islands community development program*. State, Society and Governance in Melanesia Discussion Paper, 2008/3. Canberra: SSGM, Australian National University Press.

Hills, A. (2014). What is Policeness? On being police in Somalia. *British Journal of Criminology*, No. 54, pp. 765–783.

Hoadley, S. (2011). The New Zealand PRT experience in Bamyan Province: Assessing political legitimacy and operational achievements. In *Statebuilding in Afghanistan: Multinational contributions to reconstruction*, ed. N. Hynek and P. Marton, pp. 139–156. New York: Routledge.

—— (2015). New Zealand Civil–Military Relations in Afghanistan: Aims, assessments and lessons. In *Reconstructing Afghanistan: Civil–Military Experiences in Comparative Perspective*, ed. W. Maley and S. Schmeidl, pp. 43–54. London and New York: Routledge.

Hohaia, D. (2016). In search of a decolonised military: Māori cultural learning experiences in the New Zealand Defence Force. *Kōtuitui: New Zealand Journal of Social Sciences online*, Vol. 11, No. 1, pp. 47–58.

Holmes-Eber, P. (2014). *Culture Wars: Irregular warfare, culture policy, and adaptation in the Marine Corps*. Stanford CA: Stanford University Press.

Holvino, E., B. M. Ferdman and D. Merrill-Sands (2004). Creating and Sustaining

Diversity and Inclusion in Organizations: Strategies and approaches. In *The Psychology and Management of Workplace Diversity*, ed. P. Stockdale and F. Crosby, pp. 245–276. Malden MA: Blackwell.

Honoré, A. M. (1964). Can and Can't. *Mind*, Vol. 73, No. 292, pp. 463–479.

Horn, H., K. Pepper, K. Ballantyne, C. Willan and A. Bond (2008). *Cultural Review of the Army Depot.* Wellington: NZDF.

HQNZDF CDF Minute (2013). Establishment of the NZDF Women's Development Steering Group. 5000/PB/2, dated 17 January.

Hucker, G. (2010). A determination to remember: Helen Clark and New Zealand's military heritage. *Journal of Arts Management, Law and Society*, No. 40, pp. 105–118.

Hudson, V. (2012). What Sex Means for World Peace. *Foreign Policy*, April 24. https://foreignpolicy.com/2012/04/24/what-sex-means-for-world-peace/, accessed 3 August 2016.

Huntington, S. (1957). *The Soldier and the State: The theory and politics of civil–military relations.* Harvard MA: Belknap Press.

Ignatieff, M. (2003). *Empire Lite: Nation-building in Bosnia, Kosovo and Afghanistan.* London: Vintage.

Inclusive Security (2014). *What Matters Most: Measuring plans for inclusive security.* http://www.inclusivesecurity.org/publication/matters-measuring-plans-inclusive-security/

—— (2015). *Why Women?* https://www.inclusivesecurity.org/why-women/

ISAF (2009). *ISAF Provincial Reconstruction Team (PRT) Handbook*, 4th ed. https://publicintelligence.net/isaf-provincial-reconstruction-team-prt-handbook/

Janowitz, M. (1960). *The Professional Soldier: A social and political portrait.* London: The Free Press of Glencoe Collier/Macmillan.

Jans, N. (2014). *New Values, Old Basics: How leadership shapes support for inclusion*, p. 4. Canberra: Centre for Defence and Strategic Studies, Australian Defence College.

Jans, N., with S. Mugford, J. Cullens and J. Frazer-Jans (2013). *The Chiefs: A study of strategic leadership*, p. 35. Canberra: Australian Defence College.

Jayamaha, D., S. Brady, B. Fitzgerald and J. Fritz (2010). *Lessons Learned From US Government in International Operations.* Carlisle SA: Strategic Studies Institute, US Army War College.

Johnson, D. W., and R. T. Johnson (2002). Learning Together and Alone: Overview and meta analysis. *Asia Pacific Journal of Education*, Vol. 22, No. 1, pp. 95–105.

Jonassen, D. H. (2001). Objectivism Versus Constructivism: Do we need a new philosophical paradigm? In *Classic Writings on Instructional Technology*, ed. D. Ely and T. Plomp, pp. 53–70. Englewood: Libraries Unlimited.

Jones, S. G., J. M. Wilson, A. Rathmell and K. J. Riley (2005). *Establishing Law and Order After Conflict*. Santa Monica: RAND.

Kaplan, S. (2010). Rethinking state-building in a failed state. *Washington Quarterly*, Vol. 33, No. 1, pp. 81–97.

Karim, S., and K. Beardsley (2013). Female Peacekeepers and Gender Balancing: Token gestures or informed policymaking? *International Interactions*, Vol. 39, No. 4, pp. 461–488. http://www.tandfonline.com/doi/abs/10.1080/03050629.2013.805131

Kartchner, K. (2006). *Weapons of Mass Destruction and the Crucible of Strategic Culture*. Defense Threat Reduction Agency, Advance Systems and Concepts Office. https://fas.org/irp/agency/dod/dtra/crucible.pdf

Kaufman, A. S. (1963). Ability. *Journal of Philosophy*, Vol. 60, No. 19, pp. 537–551.

Keating, T. (2014). One Force One Voice. *FORCE4NZ*, Vol. 14, No. 1, p. 2.

—— (2015a). Address by Lt. Gen. Tim Keating, Chief of Defence Force. Details of the training mission to Iraq. http://nzdf.mil.nz/downloads/pdf/general/cdf_address-iraq_training_mission.pdf, accessed 12 March 2016.

—— (2015b). 24 February. NZDF's Training Mission To Iraq. http://www.nzdf.mil.nz/news/feature-stories/2015/20150224-nzdftmti.htm, accessed 13 October 2016.

—— (2016). Cited in 2016 Women's RNZAF Development Forum. *Air Force News*, No. 178 (March), p. 15.

Keller, D. E. (2011). US Military Forces and Police Assistance in Stability Operations: The least worst option to fill the US capability gap. Carlisle SA: Strategic Studies Institute, US Army War College.

Kemp, R. (2014). Female Soldiers Just Lack the Killer Instinct. Reproduced from *The Times*, 18 November 2014. http://richard-kemp.com/female-soldiers-just-lack-the-killer-instinct/

Key, J. (2015). New Zealand Parliament Ministerial Statements, *Iraq — Deployment of Military Personnel*. 24 February, Vol. 703, p. 1813.

Kilcullen, D. (2007). Australian Statecraft: The challenge of aligning policy with strategic culture. *Security Challenges*, Vol. 3, No. 4, pp. 45–65.

King, M. (2003). *New Zealanders at War*. Auckland: Penguin.

Knowles, M. S. (1980). *The Modern Practice of Adult Education: From pedagogy to andragogy*. Chicago IL: Follett.

—— (1984). *Andragogy in Action: Applying modern principles of adult learning.* San Francisco CA: Jossey-Bass.

—— (1990). *The Adult Learner: A neglected species.* Houston TX: Gulf Publishing Co.

Kolenda, C. D. (2012). *The Counterinsurgency Challenge: A parable of leadership and decision-making in modern conflict.* Mechanicsburg PA: Stackpole Books.

Kremer, W. (2013). Captain Collette: The life of a woman on the front line. BBC World Service. http://www.bbc.com/news/magazine-24622762

Lemmon, G. (2015). A band of sisters on the special ops battlefield. CNN. http://edition.cnn.com/2015/05/23/opinions/lemmon-band-of-sisters-special-ops/

Leslie, H. (2002). Gendering conflict and conflict management in the Solomon Islands. *Development Bulletin,* No. 60, pp. 13–16.

Liebknecht, K. P. A. F. (1973). *Militarism and Anti-Militarism.* Cambridge: River Press.

Liu, J. H., T. McCreanor, T. McIntosh and T. Teaiwa (2005). Introduction: Constructing New Zealand identities. In *New Zealand Identities,* ed. J. H. Liu, T. McCreanor, T. McIntosh and T. Teaiwa, pp. 11–20. Wellington: Victoria University Press.

Loftus, B. (2010). Police Occupational Culture: Classic themes, altered times. *Policing and Society,* Vol, 20, No. 1, pp. 1–20.

McArthur, T. (2016). *NZDF Deployments.* Unpublished manuscript.

McDevitt, B. (2006). Operation Helpem Fren: A personal perspective. *Australian Army Journal,* Vol. 3, No. 2, pp. 63–80.

McGregor, J., S. Bell and M. Wilson (2015). Fault Lines: Human rights in New Zealand. New Zealand Law Foundation. http://www.aut.ac.nz/__data/assets/pdf_file/0010/536572/NO-watermark-Fault-lines-Human-rights-in-New-Zealand.pdf

McKenzie, M. (2009). Securitization and Desecuritization: Female soldiers and the reconstruction of women in post-conflict Sierra Leone. *Security Studies,* Vol. 18, No. 2, pp. 241–261.

McLeod, J. (1986). *Myth & Reality: The New Zealand soldier in World War II.* Auckland: Reed Methuen Publishers Ltd.

McMasters, H. R. (2011). *Dereliction of Duty: Lyndon Johnson, Robert McNamara, the Joint Chiefs of Staff and the lies that led to Vietnam.* New York: HarperCollins.

McNerney, M. J. (2008). CIMIC on the Edge: Afghanistan and the evolution of civil–military operations. In *Civil–Military Cooperation in Post-Conflict Operations,* ed. C. Ankersen, pp. 173–197. Abingdon: Routledge.

Malkasian, C. (2007). A Thin Blue Line in the Sand. *Democracy*, No. 5. http://www.democracyjournal.org/5/6534.php, accessed 12 January 2014.

Manawatu Standard (2001). Cadet Cavanagh following in family tradition. 29 March, p. 2.

Martin, J., ed. (2013). *The New Zealand Army: Peace support operations 1950–2013*. Wellington: New Zealand Defence Force.

—— (2014). Army psych honoured for Middle East kidnap solution. *NZ Army News*, No. 454, p. 2.

—— (2015). A New Chief of Army. *NZ Army News*, No. 466, p. 5.

Massey University (2015). Soldier's Cultural Education Key in Modern Conflicts. New Zealand Army Irregular Warfare Seminar. http://www.massey.ac.nz/massey/about-massey/news/article.cfm?mnarticle_uuid=D6D86FA3-D7E7-B2FD-1D69-66EE7D984025, accessed 13 April 2016.

Mayell, P. (2004). Beyond the 'Outer Crescent': The Mackinder century in New Zealand geopolitics. *Geographical Journal*, Vol. 170, No. 4, pp. 368–376.

MFAT (Ministry of Foreign Affairs & Trade) (2014). *Annual Report 2013/14*. Wellington. http://mfat.govt.nz/downloads/media-and-publications/annual-report/MFAT Annual Report 201314.pdf

—— (2015a). New Zealand Ranked 10th in the Latest Global Gender Gap Report. https://www.mfat.govt.nz/en/media-and-resources/news/new-zealand-ranked-10th-in-the-latest-global-gender-gap-report/

—— (2015b). New Zealand National Action Plan for the Implementation of UN Security Council Resolutions, including 1325, on Women, Peace and Security 2015–2019. https://www.mfat.govt.nz/assets/_securedfiles/ Peace-Rights-and-Security/NZ-National-Action-Plan-on-Women-Peace-and-Security.pdf

Miller, B., M. Pournik and A. Swaine (2014). Women in Peace and Security through United Nations Security Resolution 1325: Literature review, content analysis of national action plans, and implementation. Washington DC: Institute for Global and International Studies, George Washington University. http://www.peacewomen.org/assets/file/NationalActionPlans/miladpournikanalysisdocs/igis_womeninpeaceandsecuritythroughunsr1325_millerpournikswaine_2014.pdf

Ministry of Defence (2014a). Defence Assessment 2014. Wellington: MoD.

—— (2014b). Maximising Opportunities for Military Women in the New Zealand Defence Force. Evaluation Division. http://www.nzdf.mil.nz/downloads/pdf/public-docs/2014/maximising-opportunities-military-women-nzdf.pdf

—— (2016a). *New Zealand Defence White Paper*. Wellington: Ministry of Defence.

—— (2016b). Review of the Iraq Deployment. Government of New

Zealand. http://defence.govt.nz/pdfs/iraq/cab-16-sub-0112-review-of-the-iraq-deployment.pdf, accessed 16 April 2016.

Ministry of Defence/New Zealand Defence Force (2005). Briefing to the Incoming Government. www.nzdf.mil.nz/downloads/pdf/public-docs/nzdf_bim.pdf

Mobekk, E. (2010). Gender, Women and Security Sector Reform. *International Peacekeeping*, Vol. 17, No. 2, pp. 283–288.

Mockaitis, T. J. (2004). *Civil–Military Cooperation in Peace Operations: The case of Kosovo*. Carlisle SA: Strategic Studies Institute, US Army War College.

Morrison, G. R., S. M. Ross, J. E. Kemp and H. Kalman (2010). *Designing Effective Instruction*. Somerset NJ: John Wiley & Sons.

Moskos, C. (1976). *Sociology of a United Nations Military Force*. Chicago: Chicago University Press.

Moskos, C., J. A. Williams and D. R. Segal, eds (1999). *The Postmodern Military: Armed forces after the cold war*. Oxford: Oxford University Press.

Multinational Force and Observers (2014). Appointment of the MFO's Next Force Commander. 17 December. http://mfo.org/en/news/article/ appointment-of-the-mfo-s-next-force-commander, accessed 11 June 2015.

Murray, N. (2014). The role of professional military education in mission command. *Joint Force Quarterly*, No. 72 (1st quarter). St Louis MO: Universal. http://ndupress.ndu.edu/Media/News/News-Article-View/Article/577475/jfq-72-the-role-of-professional-military-education-in-mission-command/

Murray, T. (2011). Security Sector Reform in Afghanistan, 2002–2011: An overview of a flawed process. *International Studies*, Vol. 48, No. 1, pp. 43–63.

Myrttinen, H. (2009). *Poster Boys No More: Gender and security sector reform in Timor-Leste*. Geneva Centre for the Democratic Control of Armed Forces Policy Paper No. 31, Geneva: DCAF.

Nairn, K., J. Higgins and J. Sligo (2012). *Children of Rogernomics: A neoliberal generation leaves school*. Dunedin: Otago University Press.

Nanda, Dr S. (2014). The Portrayal of Women in the Fairy Tales. *International Journal of Social Sciences and Humanities Invention*, Vol. 1, No. 4, pp. 246–250. http://valleyinternational.net/thijsshi/v1-i4/7%20theijsshi.pdf

Nantais, C., and M. Lee (1999). Women in the United States Military: Protectors or protected? The case of prisoner of war Melissa Rathbun-Nealy. *Journal of Gender Studies*, Vol. 8, No. 2, pp. 181–192.

NATO (2014). NATO/EAPC Policy for the Implementation of UNSCR 1325 on Women, Peace and Security and Related Resolutions. www.nato.int/cps/en/natolive/official_texts_109830.htm

Naval Postgraduate School. https://my.nps.edu/web/ccs/bamyan, accessed July 2016.

Neikirk, A. (2009). Happily ever after (or what fairytales teach girls about being women). *Hōhōnū: A journal of academic writing*, No. 7, pp. 38–42, University of Hawai'i at Hilo. http://hilo.hawaii.edu/academics/hohonu/documents/Vol07x07HappilyEverAfter.pdf

Neudorfor, S. (2015). *Sexual Exploitation and Abuse in UN Peacekeeping: An analysis of risk and prevention factors*. London: Lexington Books.

New Zealand Aid Programme (2013). *New Zealand's Achievements from 10 Years of Development Assistance in Bamyan, Afghanistan*. Wellington: NZAP. http://www.aid.govt.nz/sites/default/files/Our Story - 10 years of development in Bamyan.pdf

New Zealand Army (2008). RAMSI: Pitching in to secure peace and stability. www.army.mil.nz/at-a-glance/mews/army-news/391/ramsi=pitspas.htm, accessed 12 August 2012.

—— (2013). *The Way of the New Zealand Warrior*. http://www.army.mil.nz/downloads/pdf/public-docs/2013/way-of-the-nz-warrior.pdf

—— (n.d.). *Combat Corps Training Soldier's Aide-Memoire*.

New Zealand Cabinet External Relations and Defence Committee (2013). *Peace Support Operations Review — ERD* Min(13) 11/3. Wellington: Cabinet Office.

New Zealand Defence Careers (2013a). Army Basic Training. http://www.defencecareers.mil.nz/army/lifestyle-salary/education-training/basic-training, accessed 20 March 2015.

—— (2013b). Army Officer. http://www.defencecareers.mil.nz/army/jobs/army-officer, accessed 20 March 2015.

New Zealand Defence Force (2009a). Statement of Intent 2009–12. http://www.nzdf.mil.nz/downloads/pdf/public-docs/2009/soi/nzdf-soi-2009-12.pdf

—— (2009b). *Leadership framework: Do more/do less matrix: Leadership level one: 'Self Leadership'*. Wellington: NZDF.

—— (2009c). *Leadership framework: Learning outcomes: Leadership level one: 'Self Leadership'*. Wellington: NZDF.

—— (2010). Statement of Intent 2010–13. http://www.nzdf.mil.nz/downloads/pdf/public-docs/2010/soi/nzdf-soi-2010-13.pdf

—— (2012). *New Zealand Defence Doctrine NZDDP-D*, 3rd ed., p. 10, para. 1.53. http://www.nzdf.mil.nz/downloads/pdf/public-docs/2012/nzddp_d_3rd_ed.pdf

—— (2013). Court of Inquiry into the Battle of Baghak. http://www.nzdf.mil.nz/downloads/pdf/public-docs/2013/coi-report_baghak_redact_reopen_final.pdf, accessed July 2016.

—— (2014). Stages of Application. http://www.defencecareers.mil.nz/army/joining-up/stages-of-application, accessed 20 May 2014.

—— (2015a). Kiwi Approach to Iraqi Training Mission. Media release. http://www.nzdf.mil.nz/news/media-releases/2015/20150401-katitm.htm, accessed 15 February 2016.

—— (2015b). On the Ground in Iraq. *FORCE4NZ*, No. 4 (October), pp. 4–5.

—— (2016a). Why do I think we need more military women? *Force4NZ*, No. 5 (February), p. 28.

—— (2016b). 'Operation RESPECT': Creating a zero tolerance approach to inappropriate behaviour. Media release, 15 March. http://www.nzdf.mil.nz/news/media-releases/2016/2016-03-15-or.htm, accessed 4 May 2016.

—— (2016c). Regular Force strength data as at 31 January 2016. Organisational Planning Systems and Development Unit.

—— (2016d). Future Afghan Army leaders complete NZDF-supported training. Media release. http://www.nzdf.mil.nz/news/media-releases/2016/20160705aalcNew Zealand.htm, accessed 18 July 2016.

—— (n.d.). Online overview. http://www.nzdf.mil.nz/about-us/governance-structure.htm#defenceact

New Zealand Government (1947). *The United Nations Report of the New Zealand Delegation on the Second Regular Session of the General Assembly Held in New York, 16 September – 29 November*, Publication No. 60. Wellington: New Zealand Government.

New Zealand Parliament (2014). *Troop Deployment Abroad: Parliamentary Consent.* www.parliament.nz/en/pb/research-papers/document/oopLLawRP2014051/troop-deployments-abroad

New Zealand Police (2015). NZ Police Code of Conduct. http://www.police.govt.nz/sites/default/files/publications/ourcode.pdf, accessed 13 October 2016.

Novak, J. D. (1998). *Learning, Creating, and Using Knowledge.* New York: Routledge.

Nowell-Smith, P. H. (1960). Ifs and Cans. *Theoria*, Vol. 26, No. 2. pp. 85–101.

Olsson, L., and T-I. Gizelis (2013). An Introduction to UNSCR 1325. *International Interactions*, No. 39, pp. 425–434. http://www.tandfonline.com/doi/abs/10.1080/03050629.2013.805327?journalCode=gini20#.VY4HwE3vq70

Ottaway, M. (2002). Rebuilding State Institutions in Collapsed States. *Development and Change*, No. 33, pp. 1001–1023.

Paina, D. (2000). Peacemaking in Solomon Islands: The experience of the Guadalcanal Women for Peace movement. *Development Bulletin*, No. 53

(November), pp. 47–48.

Panarelli, E. K. (2010). Local Ownership of Security Sector Reform. *Peacebrief*, No. 11, pp. 1–4. US Institute of Peace. https://www.usip.org/sites/default/files/PB11%20Local%20Ownership%20of%20Security%20Sector%20Reform.pdf

Pillsbury, W. B. (1938). *Psychology of Memory*. Ann Arbor MI: Edwards Brothers.

Pollard, A. (2000). Resolving conflict in Solomon Islands: The Women for Peace approach. *Development Bulletin*, No. 53 (November), pp. 44–46.

Pollock, K. (2012). Tertiary Education: Tertiary sector reform from the 1980s. In *Te Ara — The Encyclopedia of New Zealand*. http://www.teara.govt.nz/en/tertiary-education/page-4, accessed 14 March 2015.

Pring, L. (1999). Children in Armed Conflict: Girl soldiers. http://empirehistory.weebly.com/children-in-armed-conflict--girl-soldiers.html

Pruett, J. P. (2009). The Interagency Future Embedded Provincial Reconstruction Teams in Task Force Marne. *Military Review*, Vol. 89, No. 5, pp. 54–63.

Przygoda, J., and J. Chrisler (2000). Definitions of Gender and Sex: The subtleties of meaning. *Sex Roles*, Vol. 43, Nos 7/8, pp. 533–569.

Rashid, A. (2000). *Taliban: Militant Islam, oil and fundamentalism in Central Asia*. Yale: Yale University Press.

Reardon, L. (2010). Assessing Adult Learning: literacy and numeracy competencies. Panel session, conference proceedings, August. http://www. nzcer.org.nz/system/files/Assessing_adult_learning_conference_proceedings2010.pdf, accessed 14 February 2016.

Reigeluth, C. (1999). *Instructional-design theories and models: A new paradigm of instructional theory*, Vol. II. Mahwah NJ: Lawrence Erlbaum Associates.

Richmond, O. P. (2011). *A Post-Liberal Peace*. London: Routledge.

Reveron, D. S. (2010). *Exporting Security: International engagement, security cooperation and the changing face of the US military*. Washington: Georgetown University Press.

Ritchie, J. (2001). Not everything can be reduced to numbers. In *Health Research*, ed. C. Berglund, pp. 149–173. Melbourne: Oxford University Press.

Robinson, L. (2008). *Tell Me How This Ends: General David Petraeus and the search for a way out of Iraq*. New York: Public Affairs.

Rolfe, J. (1999). *The Armed Forces of New Zealand*. New South Wales: Allen & Unwin.

—— (2001). Peacekeeping the Pacific Way in Bougainville. *International Peacekeeping*, Vol. 8, No. 4, pp. 38–55.

—— (2015). Armed Forces — Historical Overview. In *Te Ara — The Encyclopedia of New Zealand.* http://www.teara.govt.nz/en/graph/35716/defence-force-personnel-by-gender-and-ethnicity-2012, accessed 7 August 2016.

Royal Military Academy Sandhurst (2014). *ANAOA Coalition Force Mentor Course 21–30 May 2014.* London: British Army.

Rubinstein, R. A. (2012). Ethical Considerations from the Study of Peacekeeping. In *Anthropologists in the SecurityScape: Ethics, practice, and professional identity,* ed. R. Albro, G. Marcus, L. A. McNamara and M. Schoch-Spana, pp. 183–195. Walnut Creek CA: Left Coast Press Inc.

Ryan, G. W., and H. R. Bernard (2003). Techniques to Identify Themes. *Field Methods,* Vol. 15, No. 1, pp. 85–109.

Ryan, S. (2014). The gender gap: How NZ is faring. *NZ Herald Online,* 29 October. http://www.nzherald.co.nz/business/news/article.cfm?c_id=3&objectid=11349638

Sacks, H. (1972). Notes on police assessment of moral character. In *Studies in Social Interaction,* ed. D. Sudnow, pp. 280–292. New York: Free Press.

Salas, E., and J. A. Cannon-Bowers (2001). The Science of Training: A decade of progress. *Annual Review of Psychology,* Vol. 52, No. 1, pp. 471–499.

Sales, L. (2015). Create the society you want to live in. ABC. www.abc.net.au/7.30/content/2015/s4233807.htm

Sanghera, G., M. Henry and P. Higate (2008). *Peacekeepers as New Men? Security and masculinity in the United Nations Mission in Liberia.* SPAIS Working paper 02-08, School of Sociology, Politics, and International Studies, University of Bristol. https://scholar.google.co.uk/citations?view_op=view_citation&hl=en&user=I9yC9gUAAAAJ&citation_for_view=I9yC9gUAAAAJ:MXK_kJrjxJIC

Sannerholm, R. Z. (2013). Re-Conceptualisations Should Be Uncomfortable: Comments on 'The Justice-Security-Development Nexus: Theory and practice in fragile and conflict-affected states' by Doug Porter, Deborah Isser and Louis-Alexandre Berg. *Hague Journal on the Rule of Law,* Vol. 5, No. 2, pp. 329–333.

Schiff, R. (2009). *The Military and Domestic Politics: A concordance theory of civil–military relations.* London and New York: Routledge.

Schnabel, A., and M. Krupanski (2012). *Mapping Evolving Internal Roles of the Armed Forces,* SSR Paper 7. Geneva: DCAF.

Scoppio, G. (2010). Indigenous Peoples in the New Zealand Defence Force and the Canadian Forces. *Canadian Military Journal,* Vol. 10, No. 4, pp. 36–45. http://www.journal.forces.gc.ca/vol10/no4/07-scoppio-eng.asp

Scott, J. W. (1971). RTC Retreat. In *The American Military,* ed. M. Oppenheimer. Somerset NJ: Transaction.

Scrimshaw, K. (2014). New Zealand Association for Training Development. #New Zealandatd14 21 Oct14. https://twitter.com/kariscrimshaw, accessed 10 April 2016.

Seal, G. (2007). ANZAC: The sacred in the secular. *Journal of Australian Studies*, Vol. 31, No. 91, pp. 135–144.

Seck. H. H. (2016). Opening combat jobs to women will mean lower standards: Marine general. http://www.military.com/daily-news/2016/01/08/opening-combat-jobs-women-mean-lower-standards-marine-general.html

Sedra, M. (2010). Introduction: The Future of Security Sector Reform. In *The Future of Security Sector Reform*, ed. M. Sedra. Ontario: Centre for International Governance Innovation. https://www.cigionline.org/sites/default/files/the_future_of_security_sector_reform.pdf

Sharp, I. (2013). Feminist Peace Activism 1915 and 2010: Are we nearly there yet? *Peace and Change: A journal of peace research*, Vol. 38, No. 2, pp. 155–180. http://www.researchgate.net/publication/264508517_Feminist_Peace_Activism_1915_and_2010_Are_We_Nearly_There_Yet

Simic, O. (2012). *Regulation of Sexual Conduct in UN Peacekeeping Operations.* New York: Springer.

Simons, A. (2012). How Critical Should Critical Thinking Be? Teaching soldiers in wartime. In *Anthropologists in the SecurityScape: Ethics, practice, and professional identity*, ed. R. Albro, G. Marcus, L. A. McNamara and M. Schoch-Spana, pp. 231–243. Walnut Creek CA: Left Coast Press Inc.

Simons, M. (2001). *New Zealand's Continued Contribution to UNTSO.* Unpublished manuscript.

Sjoberg, L. (2013). *Gender, War and Conflict.* London: Polity.

Spector, J. M. (2000). Gagné's Influence on Military Training Research and Development. In *The Legacy of Robert M. Gagné*, ed. R. Richey, pp. 211–227. New York: ERIC-IT Clearing House.

Spencer, E. (2010). *Solving the People Puzzle: Cultural intelligence and special operations forces.* Toronto: Dundurn Press.

Starren, A., Luijters, K., Drupsteen, L., Vilevicius, G. and L. Eeckelaert (2013). *Diverse Cultures at Work: Ensuring safety and health through leadership and participation.* Luxembourg: European Agency for Safety and Health at Work.

State Services Commission, the Treasury and the Department of the Prime Minister and Cabinet (2012). *Formal Review of the New Zealand Police (Police).* Wellington: Performance Improvement Framework. https://www.ssc.govt.nz/sites/all/files/pif-police-review-sept12.PDF, accessed 11 October 2016.

—— (2015). *Review of the New Zealand Defence Force (NZDF)*. Wellington: Performance Improvement Framework. https://www.ssc.govt.nz/sites/all/files/pif-nzdf-review-sep15_0.pdf, accessed 10 August 2016.

Steer, Rear Admiral J., Chief of Navy (2014). Warriors of the Sea — Te Taua Moana initiative launched. http://www.navy.mil.nz/nap/nn/warriors-of-the-sea-te-taua-moana-initiative-launched.htm

Sullivan, G. R. (2010). Today's training and education (development) revolution: The future is now. *Land Warfare Papers*, No. 76 (April), p. v.

Sultana, F. (2014). By whose words shall we know and to what end? Genealogies and its others in geography. *Dialogues in Human Geography*, Vol. 4, No. 3, pp. 335–338.

Swain, R. (2005). *Changes In Instructional System Design (ISD): Improving Training Product Delivery To United States Army Soldiers.* Carlisle Barracks PA: US Army War College.

Swaine, A. (2009). Assessing the Potential of National Action Plans to Advance Implementation of United Nations Security Council Resolution 1325. *Yearbook of International Humanitarian Law*, Vol. 12.

Sylvester, C., ed. (2011). *Experiencing War*. New York: Routledge.

Tabor, A. (2016). How to prepare for Building Partner Capacity: Culture. Presentation at the Defence Engagement Symposium held at NZ Army Linton Military Camp, Palmerston North, May.

Tan, M. (2015). First female 4-star shares lessons in 'A Higher Standard'. *Army Times*, 19 May. http://www.armytimes.com/story/military/careers/army/officer/2015/05/19/gen-dunwoody-new-leadership-book/27179551/

Taylor-Doig, K. (2013). The NZDF in Bamyan. *NZ Army News*, No. 441, pp. 2–11.

Teaiwa, T. (2008). Globalizing and Gendered Forces: The contemporary militarization of Pacific/Oceania. In *Gender and Globalization in Asia and the Pacific: Method, practice, theory*, ed. K. E. Ferguson and M. Mironesco, pp. 318–332. Honolulu: University of Hawai'i Press.

The Press (1999). Army's tertiary schemes. 6 September, p. 43.

Tomlinson, H., and S. Frenkel (2013). Cairo to seek Israeli assent for strike on Sinai jihadists. *The Times*, 11 July. http://www.thetimes.co.uk/tto/news/world/middleeast/article3813393.ece, accessed 12 August 2012.

UK Ministry of Defence (2009). *A Guide to Joint Doctrine Publication 3-40: Security and Stabilisation: The military contribution*, November. https://www.gov.uk/ government/uploads/system/uploads/attachment_data/file/43332/jdp340guideweb.pdf, accessed 13 July 2013.

UN Women (n.d.). Gender Mainstreaming. www.unwomen.org/en/how-we-work/un-system-coordination/gender-mainstreaming

United Nations (2016). Gender Statistics by Mission, February. Includes military expert, troops and police. http://www.un.org/en/peacekeeping/resources/statistics/gender.shtml

United Nations Department of Peacekeeping Operations (2005a). *United Nations Police: Building Institutional Police Capacity in Post-Conflict Environments.* New York: UN DPKO.

—— (2005b). *Gender and UN Peacekeeping Operations.* New York: UN DPKO.

United Nations Development Programme (2009). *Capacity Development: A primer.* New York: UNDP.

—— (2014). *Iraqi Human Development Report 2014. Iraqi Youth: Challenges and opportunities,* pp. 84–102. Iraq: Ministry of Planning and Baytal Hikma. http://www.iq.undp.org/content/dam/iraq/img/Publications/UNDP-IQ_IraqNHDR2014-English.pdf, accessed 7 February 2016.

United Nations Education, Scientific and Cultural Organization (2012). *Adult and Youth Literacy, 1990–2015. Analysis of data for 41 Selected Countries.* Montreal, Canada: UNESCO Institute for Statistics.

United Nations Institute for Training and Research (1997). What is Capacity Building? Online-Resource Centre, UNITAR. http://www2.unitar.org/dfm/Resource_Center/Links/CapacityBuilding.htm#a, accessed 20 March 2014.

United Nations Security Council, *Security Council Resolution 1325* (2000), 31 October 2000, S/RES/1325 (2000). http://www.un.org/en/sc/documents/resolutions/

United Nations Trust Fund for Human Security (2014). *Human Security Unit Strategic Plan 2014–2017.* https://docs.unocha.org/sites/dms/HSU/HSU%20Strategic%20Plan%202014-2017%20Web%20Version.pdf

Urlich, S. (2011). Operation RUA. *NZ Army News,* No. 423, pp. 16–17.

US Army (2008). *FM 3-07 Stability Operations.* Washington DC: Headquarters Department of the Army.

US Army Marine Corps (2007). *Counterinsurgency Field Manual, US Army Field Manual No. 3-24 / Marine Corps Warfighting Publication No. 3-33.5.* Chicago and London: University of Chicago Press.

US Joint Chiefs of Staff (2010). *Joint Publication 3-22: Foreign Internal Defence.* Washington DC: Department of Defense.

Vuga, J., and J. Juvan (2013). Inside the Military Organization: Experience of researching the Slovenian armed forces. In *Qualitative Methods in Military Studies,* ed. H. C. C. Castro, pp. 116–132. Abingdon: Routledge.

Wainwright, E. (2003). Responding to state failure — the case of Australia and the Solomon Islands. *Australian Journal of International Affairs*, Vol. 57, No. 3 (November), pp. 485–498.

Wallace, D. (2016). The air force marae update. *Air Force News*, No. 181 (June), pp. 20–21.

Watson, T. J. (2008). Managing Identity: Identity work, personal predicaments and structural circumstances. *Organization*, Vol. 15, No. 1, pp. 121–143.

Webb, D. (2016). First Word. *Air Force News*, No. 179, p. 3.

Wesley, M. (2008). The State of the Art on the Art of State Building. *Global Governance*, Vol. 14, No. 3 (July/September), pp. 369–385.

Westendorf, J-K. (2013). 'Add Women and Stir': The Regional Assistance Mission to Solomon Islands and Australia's implementation of United Nations Security Council Resolution 1325. *Australian Journal of International Affairs*, Vol. 67, No. 4, pp. 456–474.

Wheeler, M. (2011). *Land Component Commander Directive: Reconfiguration of the Kippenberger Scheme*. Waiouru, New Zealand: Officer Cadet School.

Whitworth, S. (2004). *Men, Militarism and UN Peacekeeping: A gendered analysis*. Boulder CO: Lynne Rienner Publishers.

—— (2005). Militarized Masculinities and the Politics of Peacekeeping: The Canadian case. In *Critical Security Studies and World Politics*, ed. K. Booth, pp. 89–106. Boulder CO: Lynne Rienner Publishers.

van Wijk, C. H., and G. Finchilescu (2008). Symbols of Organisational Culture: Describing and prescribing gender integration of navy ships. *Journal of Gender Studies*, Vol. 17, No. 3, pp. 237–249. http://www.tandfonline.com/doi/abs/10.1080/09589230802204266

Willett S. (2010). Introduction. Security Council Resolution 1325: Assessing the impact on women, peace and security. *International Peacekeeping*, Vol. 17, No. 2, pp. 142–158. http://www.tandfonline.com/doi/abs/10.1080/13533311003625043#.VZ8Nm03vq70

Wineera, J. (2014). Training us to train them. Observations of New Zealand military advisors preparing to train Afghan Army officer cadets. Poster by author.

Winslow, D. (2005). Strange Bedfellows in Humanitarian Crises: NGOs and the military. In *Twisting Arms and Flexing Muscles: Humanitarian intervention and peacebuilding in perspective*, ed. T. M. Shaw and N. Mychajlyszyn. Aldershot: Ashgate.

Zhang, Y., and B. M. Wildemuth (2009). Qualitative analysis of content. In *Applications of Social Research Methods to Questions in Information and Library Science*, ed. B. Wildemuth, pp. 308–319. Westport CT: Libraries Unlimited.

About the contributors

LIEUTENANT COLONEL JANE DERBYSHIRE has been a member of the New Zealand Defence Force since 1997. She has served as an artillery officer and a legal officer. Lt Col Derbyshire practised as a lawyer for 12 years, with her last legal post as the Chief Legal Advisor at NZDF's operational headquarters. As part of her military career she taught at Massey University in the law of armed conflict and military law. Her current role is a Deputy Director of HR strategy, responsible for HR policy and organisational research. She has a Master's in International Security, a Bachelor of Laws and a Bachelor of Commerce majoring in economics.

W. J. FISH is Professor of Philosophy at Massey University, and co-author of *Internal Security and Statebuilding: Aligning Agencies and Functions* (Routledge 2015). In addition to his research on the interaction between police and military, he has also taught ethics in senior officer courses at the NZDF Command and Staff College.

B. K. GREENER is Associate Professor, Politics Programme at Massey University. She has regularly taught senior and intermediate officer and Warrant Officer courses at the NZDF Command and Staff College since 2004, and been actively involved in the UN Police Division's International Policing Advisory Council. Dr Greener has published numerous book chapters on international security issues as well as authoring articles in journals such as *International Peacekeeping, Policing and Society, Journal of Peacebuilding and Development, Small Wars and Insurgencies* and *International Relations*, amongst others. Previous books include *The New International Policing* (Palgrave 2009) and *Internal Security and Statebuilding: Aligning Agencies and Functions* (Routledge 2015) — the latter being co-authored with W. J. Fish. Forthcoming projects include a co-edited book with Dr Anna Powles on regulating private security providers in the Pacific, work on civil–military relations in peace operations, issues in gender and policing, and post-conflict statebuilding.

DR PETER GREENER is a Senior Fellow at the Centre for Strategic Studies, Victoria University of Wellington, and an Honorary Professor at the Command and Staff College of the NZDF, where he was previously Academic Dean and has taught since 2008. Peter is also an Adjunct Professor at AUT University, where he was Head of the School of Public Health and Psychosocial Studies (2003–7) and Head of the Department of Psychotherapy and Applied Psychology (1998–2003). Peter's PhD is in political studies with a focus on New Zealand defence decision-making, and he writes regularly on capability developments in the New Zealand Defence Force.

MAIKE GUESGEN is a graduate student in social anthropology at Massey University. Maike holds a Postgraduate Diploma in Arts, with experience in military anthropology and research interests in identity, self and neoliberalism.

DR NINA HARDING recently completed her PhD in social anthropology at Massey University. In order to examine the transition from civilian to soldier, she was embedded with a cohort of new soldiers for the first year and a half of their careers in the New Zealand Army, from their first day of basic training to their first overseas deployment with the Regional

Assistance Mission to the Solomon Islands. Her previous research includes a Master's thesis based on the deployment stories of Royal New Zealand Air Force veterans of the 1991 Persian Gulf War.

DR MICHAEL LAUREN is a research leader at the Defence Technology Agency in Auckland, which is part of the New Zealand Defence Force. He works in the areas of military operational analysis and mathematical modelling, and has conducted numerous analytical studies for the Defence Force, visiting operations in both Afghanistan and Timor-Leste. His work on using agent-based combat models to analyse current and future operations has appeared in many journal articles and books. He holds a PhD in physics from the University of Auckland.

SAMANTHA MORRIS recently graduated from Victoria University, Wellington, with a Master of Development Studies, supported by a scholarship from the Peace and Disarmament Education Trust (PADET NZ). Her research focuses primarily on the intersection of security and development in conflict and post-conflict environments, and more specifically on the role of military actors in this space. She is currently employed as a Wellington-based staff member for Volunteer Service Abroad (VSA).

CAMERON SIGLEY has been a member of the New Zealand Police for 20 years. Since 2009 he has been continuously involved in the international policing environment. This included being part of a peacekeeping contingent in Timor-Leste and Afghanistan, and as a United Nations seconded police advisor, firstly to the United Nations Integrated Mission in Timor-Leste (UNMIT) for two years and then at the Department of Peacekeeping Operations (DPKO), New York, principally in the areas of community policing and sex and gender-based violence. Since returning to New Zealand he has been involved in work with the UN DPKO, the United

Nations Development Programme and UN Women, working primarily in policing development.

KIRI STEVENS is a policy advisor at the New Zealand Ministry of Foreign Affairs and Trade. The research for her chapter occurred while she was studying towards her Master of Development Studies in 2011–12. Her fieldwork in the Solomon Islands looked at how involvement in peacekeeping is changing the skills valued in the New Zealand Defence Force from a gendered perspective, with a particular focus on masculinities.

LIEUTENANT COLONEL JOSH WINEERA is a career officer in the New Zealand Army. He is currently serving in the Directorate of Strategic Engagement, specialising in the Asia-Pacific region, and he is also the Defence Advisor Pacific. Lt Col Wineera has deployed on active service to the Middle East, South East Asia and the Pacific. He has taught military tactics in Australia, and from 2010–13 was seconded to Massey University as a lecturer in military operations and irregular warfare. In 2012 he was selected by the State Department to study US National Security Policymaking. He is a track-two international security expert with the Council for Security Cooperation in the Asia-Pacific and the Asia New Zealand Foundation. Lt Col Wineera is currently undertaking part-time doctoral study with the University of Otago, examining the field of training local indigenous security forces. His work has been published in the United States, the United Kingdom and New Zealand.

Acknowledgements

BETH GREENER would like to thank all the serving men and women who have given her their time and input over the past few years. 'You are too many to list, but I would like those who have provided access, feedback, tea and biscuits or lifts in vehicles and aircraft to know they are appreciated.'

PETER GREENER would like to thank Brigadier (retd) Mark Wheeler and Captain Shaun Fogarty for supporting the initial research concept; Major General Dave Gawn and Air Vice-Marshall Kevin Short for their support when each, as Commander Joint Forces New Zealand, made possible his visits to missions, and all of the New Zealand Senior National Officers and participating officers in those missions who helped make this research possible.

MAIKE GUESGEN would like to thank the former members of the Kippenberger scheme who participated in the interviews and took time to share their experience of military life; Dr Robyn Andrews and Dr Carolyn Morris, who supervised the project and provided guidance and mentoring through the writing process. Special thanks go to Dr Beth Greener for providing the opportunity for young academics to share their research with a wider audience through the publication of this book.

MICHAEL LAUREN would like to thank Major General Dave Gawn for proposing the visit to Bamiyan that made this work possible; all the members of the Joint Forces New Zealand and OPCRIB who facilitated and participated in this study; and Louisa O'Brien and Peter Greener for the helpful discussions.

SAMANTHA MORRIS would like to thank the NZDF personnel who kindly gave their time to share their reflections with her during her research.

KIRI STEVENS thanks her supervisors Carol Harrington and Sara Kindon, and the two scholarships through which she received support: the Asia Pacific Research Award and the White Poppy Peace Scholarship.